To u
love always Nick and
JACQUELINE

2

BEER-DRINKIN'
4-WHEELIN'
HELL-RAISIN'
ARROW-SHOOTIN'
SLUG-SLINGIN'

VENISON

COOKBOOK

Rick Black

© 2001, Rick Black

All rights reserved. No part of this book may be reproduced or transmitted in any form or by any means, electronic or mechanical, including photocopying, recording or by any informational storage or retrieval system, except by a reviewer who may quote brief passages in a review to be printed in a magazine or newspaper - without permission in writing from the publisher.

DEDICATION

This Book is dedicated to my loving wife, Becky Black. For 16 years she has put up with my obsession with deer hunting. Every year my buddies and I come up with some hair brain ideas that will land us the world record buck. Now my son Travis has joined the hunting party. This year he and I shot 8-pointers side by side. This year my son became a deer-hunting nut also. Every year Becky is up at 3:00am getting us ready for the hunt. She doesn't ask for much, just the normal stuff like; don't shoot yourself, try to breath threw your nose, don't get lost and bring lots of toilet paper.
My wife makes me want to be a better man.

Preface

This is not your run of the mill wild game cookbook. A beer drinking, 4 wheeling, hell raising, arrow shooting and slug slinging deer hunter wrote this book. The reader will discover the fine art of cooking venison along with some of the funniest deer hunting stories on paper. This book was 16 years in the making and will be enjoyed by the readers for many more.

This book was written to be shared by deer hunter's and their family and friends.

The Truth About Beer And Deer

Billy and Rick went to the bar one afternoon. Billy was explaining his theory about beer and deer to his buddy Rick. And here's how it went:

" Well, you see Rick; it's like this...a herd of deer can only move as fast as the slowest deer. And when the herd is hunted, it is the slowest and weakest ones at the back that are killed first.

This natural selection is good for the herd as a whole, because the general speed and health of the whole group keeps improving by the regular killing of the weakest members.

In much the same way, the human brain can only operate as fast as the slowest brain cells. Excessive intake of beer, as we all know, kills brain cells, but naturally it attacks the slowest and weakest brain cells first.

In this way, regular consumption of beer eliminates the weaker brain cells, making the brain faster and more efficient. And that's why you always feel smarter after kicking back a few beers."

12

Introduction

If I only had a dollar for every time I heard the sound of my wife's voice screaming *you ain't cooking that deer meat in my house!* Yep it was the same thing every year, I would spend the week with my buddies deep in the heart of deer camp, grunting and snorting while sitting around the fire talking about the day's hunt.

Deer hunting with us was not a sport. It was a way of life handed down by our midwestern forefathers. The only problem was that the foremothers didn't hand it down to their daughters. Thus caused what I now refer to as the " Please don't yell at me in front of my posse" syndrome that took place every year. So how did I get my lovely bride of sixteen years to overcome her yearly dislike of my manly meat? The answer was with facts. Some examples; Did you know that the finest chefs and cooks serve up medallions of venison braised with sauce perigourdine and merlot in some of the best restaurants in the world? And they get paid big bucks for it because they know how to cook it properly to maximize the great venison flavor.

Venison is much leaner than beef and has not been subject to all of the growth chemicals. There are several things we must first know about venison to ensure a great cooking experience. I strongly feel it begins with the preparation of the deer meat. Venison is difficult meat to cook correctly. It is very important to shoot the deer, as quickly and cleanly as possible, this will affect the final quality of the meat. It is also a must to cool the meat as quickly as possible. Get the innards outwards as quickly as possible and wash and/or wipe the carcass down with a towel.

If you have to field transport, leave the skin on, but get it off as soon as you possibly can. A carcass left at blood temperature will quickly sour and ruin good meat, and getting the skin off helps heat to dissipate. Ice or snow can be helpful, but be aware that moisture is not a good thing in general for deer meat, so you want to keep it dry if possible as well as cold. As far as processing your deer meat, I would recommend seeking out a meat locker or butcher to do this for you. I highly recommend this for first time deer hunters. Now, we all have buddies that every year turn their garage into a "do it yourself" meat locker, and I have been known to wrap a hundred lbs of burger in fifteen minutes or less, but this all takes time and experience.

Now that I'm older and wiser I let the butcher do the task. When I get my meat back it is cut, wrapped and already frozen. Thus my wife does not need to seek therapy for walking in on me and the boy's drinking beer and eating chili in a blood soaked garage. Again, have the butcher do it and buy a new quad runner with the money you will save from not having to pay the therapist.

I love deer hunting and I love cooking especially my own game. I can't think of a better time than getting family and friends together to enjoy the fruits of our hunt. I so much enjoy teaching my son the art of deer hunting and the manly art of cooking venison.

I hope you take time and try many of these tasty recipes. Remember deer hunting is very enjoyable and you will always have a great time from the timber to the table.

- **Rick Black**

Soups and Stews

When it comes to the cold days and chilly nights of a midwest winter, I can't think of a more enjoyable experience than the aroma of a good soup or stew cooking in a Dutch oven. Many of hunters have came home or back to deer camp to sit around a wood burning stove with a pot of chili on top. You can taste the love and pride in each spoonful of good soup.

I have put together some of my favorite soup and stew recipes. Although you may find several types of soups with similar names such as "chili", please read each one, because each will have it's own flavor and each is truly delicious.

Remember soup should be as much fun to make as it is to eat, so make sure and try them all with friends and family!

Barbecued Beans and Venison	36
Becky's Quick Venison Stew	24
Billy's Big Buck Stew	22
Bubba's Venison Stew	23
Buck Eve Chili	40
Buck Trail Chili	34
Chuck Wagon Venison Soup	41
Dad's Favorite Deer Chili	28
Deer Camp Chili	21
Deer Soup Stock	38
Deer Spaghetti Sauce	37
El'Blackies Venison Taco Soup	31
John's Venison Hash	35
Mike's Trooper Venison Stew	20
Shaena's Ham, Venison and Bean Soup	32
Travis' Slow Cooker Venison Stew	19
Venison And Barley Soup	26
Venison Stew, Basque Style	30
Venison Soup With Cream Of Mushroom And Celery	25
Venison Stewed In Beer	29
Yankee Venison Stew	27

Travis's Slow Cooker Venison Stew –

- 3 lbs. Venison
- 6 medium potatoes
- 5 carrots
- 3 stalks of celery
- 1 large onion
- 2 cloves garlic
- 10 brown bouillon cubes

Cut venison into 1inch chunks. Roll in flour until coated all around. Cube potatoes, carrots, celery, onions and garlic. Brown venison in oil until half brown. Add 10 bouillon cubs and 3 cups of hot water to skillet and simmer for 2 minutes.

Scrape meat and gravy from skillet and add to slow cooker. Add all vegetables and stir together with meat and add 3 more cups of hot water. Cook on high for six hours. Add cornstarch to thicken as needed.

Why do they call it the Department of Interior when they are in charge of everything outdoors?

Mike's Trooper Venison Stew-

- 1 lb. Venison stew meat (1 inch chunks)
- 1 can beefy mushroom soup
- 4 medium potatoes chopped into thirds
- 2 chopped carrots
- 1 small onion
- ½ cup water
- 1 package of buttermilk biscuits

Place the meat in a crock-pot and set on low heat. Add vegetables to meat. Pour the soup over the mixture and add ½ cup of water. Cover and allow cooking for 8 hours.

Before serving, prepare biscuits. Serve stew over the biscuits.

Deer Camp Chili –

- 5 table spoons of bacon drippings
- 3 lbs of ground venison
- 2 large chopped onions
- 3 minced garlic cloves
- 2 chopped bell peppers
- 3 chopped jalapeno peppers
- 2 cans tomatoes
- 16 oz tomato sauce
- 1 tablespoon ground cumin
- 1 tablespoon paprika
- 1 cup water
- 32 oz chili beans
- 1 shot whiskey

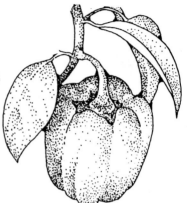

Heat bacon drippings in a large heavy pot. Add meat and cook until slightly browned. Add onions, garlic, bell peppers, jalapeno peppers and sauté until limp. Add tomatoes, tomato sauce, chili powder, cumin, paprika, whiskey, salt and pepper. Stir to blend.

Add water and simmer about 30 minutes. Add beans and continue to cook about 45 more minutes.

Once Billy and Bubba were driving down the road when they come across a Deer Crossing sign. This was when Billy says; I wonder how they get them deer to cross at that yellow sign?

Billy's Big Buck Stew –

- 4 lbs of bite sized venison
- flour
- 5 tablespoon bacon fat
- ½ cup hot water
- 1 cup dry red wine
- 1 basil
- 1 tablespoon dried parsley
- 1 large onion
- ½ tablespoon salt
- 1 tablespoon garlic powder
- 1 teaspoon red pepper
- 4 carrots, scraped/quartered
- 5 potatoes, scraped/quartered
- 1 tablespoon onion powder

Warm bacon fat in a large pot. Roll venison in flour until venison is well coated. Brown the venison in bacon fat, wine, herbs, onions, salt and pepper.

Cover and bring to boil. Lower heat and simmer two hours. Add carrots and potatoes. Cover and simmer 1 hour, adding more hot water if needed.

When meat is tender and the vegetables are done, serve with French bread.

Bubba's Venison Stew –

- 4 lbs of venison cut into bite size chunks
- 4 medium diced and sautéed onions
- 4 potatoes, diced
- 8 cups beef broth
- ½ cup real butter
- 8 ounces cream style corn
- 16 oz can of lima beans
- 1 can peeled tomatoes
- 1 tablespoon Tabasco
- 2 tablespoon Worcestershire sauce
- 2 bay leaves
- 2 tablespoon garlic powder
- 2 tablespoon salt
- 1 tablespoon peppercorns
- 1 tablespoon dried red pepper

Roll venison chunks in flour. In a large add oil and brown venison chunks. When the meat is brown add all the listed ingredients and simmer slowly for about an hour with the pot covered.

When the meat is tender, check if seasoning adjustment is needed. Add water if required. Serve this stew in soup bowls with buttermilk biscuits.

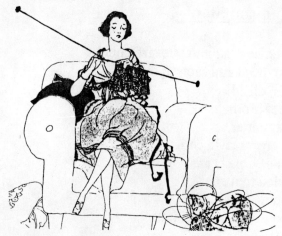

Becky's Quick Venison Stew –

- 4 lbs venison (bite sized chunks)
- 1 large onion
- 4 medium potatoes
- 5 carrots
- 2 cans cream of mushroom soup
- 1 tablespoon garlic powder
- 1 tablespoon pepper
- 1 tablespoon salt

Cut up carrots, onions and potatoes. Add two cans of cream of mushroom soup plus two cans of water and add all ingredients to crock pot, mix, and turn on medium heat for eight hours.

Stir occasionally. Serve with bread and butter.

" Old deer hunters never die, they just stay loaded"

Venison soup with cream of mushroom and celery –

- 1 onion
- 4 carrots, chopped
- 2 lbs venison (bite sized chunks)
- 1 pound boneless pork loin, cubed
- 1 tablespoon salt
- 1 tablespoon white sugar
- 1 pint water
- 1 tablespoon Worcestershire sauce
- 1 table dry red pepper
- 1 can cream of mushroom soup
- 1 can cream of celery soup

Add onion, carrots, venison, pork, salt, sugar, Worcestershire, and water to crock-pot. Cook for 30 minutes. Add cream of mushroom soup and cream of celery soup.

Cook for 4 hours, stirring when needed. Serve with rice.

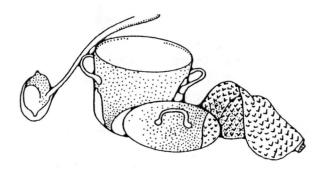

Venison and Barley soup –

- 2 deer shanks
- 1 cup barley, pearl
- 1 cup peas, green split
- 2 onions, chopped
- 2 garlic clove, finely chopped
- 1 bell pepper, seeded, chopped
- 14 cups beef stock
- 5 tablespoons butter
- 2 tablespoon salt
- 1 tablespoon pepper
- 1 bay leaf

Brown garlic, onion and pepper in butter. Add venison, cut into 1-inch pieces and brown lightly. Add stock and remaining ingredients and bring to a boil.

Cover and simmer for 2-3 hours, until meat is tender. Season according to taste.

Yankee Venison Stew –

- 4 lbs cubed venison
- 1 cup diced onion
- 14 diced potatoes
- 5 diced carrots
- 1 pack frozen vegetables
- 1 cup chopped celery
- ½ cup barley
- 9 cups water
- 2 tablespoon salt
- 3 tablespoon garlic powder
- 1 tablespoon pepper
- 1 tablespoon dry parsley
- 1 table beef soup base
- 1 package brown gravy mix
- 1 bay leaf

Sear venison until brown on all sides. Add water. Add celery, carrots, potatoes, onions and all other ingredients except frozen veggies.

Cook on medium until vegetables are tender and meat is cooked through.

Add frozen veggies and cook until hot. Serve with buttermilk biscuits.

Bud: why do you go hunting without bullets? Bubba: Because it is cheaper and the results are the same.

Dad's Favorite Deer Chili –

- 2 lbs deer burger
- 1 chopped yellow onion
- 1 diced yellow bell pepper
- 1 diced red bell pepper
- 3 chopped garlic cloves
- 1 large can chopped tomatoes
- 1 can kidney beans
- 1 can pinto beans
- 4 tablespoons tomato paste
- ½ cup red wine
- 4 tablespoons olive oil
- 1 tablespoon ground cumin
- 2 tablespoons chili powder
- 1 tablespoon Tabasco

Heat olive oil in a large Dutch oven. Sauté chopped onions and garlic. Add deer burger and cook until no longer red. Add chopped bell peppers and sauté for approximately 10 minutes. Add canned tomatoes, beans, tomato paste, wine and spices. Simmer on stove top on low for at least two hours. Salt and pepper to taste. Serve with grated Gruyere cheese and chopped onions.

Venison Stewed In Beer –

- 4 lbs of venison cut in bite size chunks
- ½ cup all purpose flour
- 4 tablespoons of butter
- 5 shallots, minced
- 1 bottle of beer, at room temperature
- 1 bay leaf
- 1 tablespoon thyme
- ½ pint sour cream
- 1 teaspoon onion powder
- 1 teaspoon garlic salt

Roll venison chunks in all-purpose flour. Add floured meat in oil and fry until all sides are brown. Do this in a large pot. Add shallots while meat is browning.

Reduce heat and pour the beer into the pan. Add bay leaf and thyme. Cook covered over moderate heat until meat is tender.

When meat is tender, raise the heat until the liquid is just short of boiling; stir in the sour cream. Stir until the liquid is smooth and add onion and garlic powder.

Salt and pepper to taste. Serve with rice or hard rolls.

A good deer hunter will always dim his headlights for approaching vehicles, even if the gun is loaded, and the deer is in sight.

Venison Stew, Basque Style –

- 5 slices bacon, diced
- 2 tablespoons butter
- ¾ pound small pearl onions, peeled
- 2 lbs venison cut in bite size chunks
- 2 cloves minced garlic
- 2 tablespoon flour
- 2 cups dry red wine
- 1 tablespoon salt
- ½ tablespoon pepper
- ¼ cup brandy
- ½ bay leaf

In a heavy stew – pot, sauté the bacon bits in the butter until they are translucent. Add the onions and cook until they are lightly browned, stirring often. Remove the bacon bits and onion leaving as much fat in the pan as possible and set them aside.

Put the venison pieces in the pan and cook with frequent stirring. Add wine, salt, pepper, bay leaf and return the bacon bits and onions to the pan.

Bring to a boil, reduce heat, and simmer for about an hour, until meat is tender. Stir in the brandy, let simmer while stirring for four minutes.

Serve with crusty bread.

Bubba gets lost in the woods while deer hunting, so he does the standard survival procedure of firing three shots into the air. Every few hours, he repeats this, but no one comes.

Finally after two days, someone stumbles across him. "Boy am glad to see you! He shouts, I ran out of arrows about three hours ago"

El`Blackies Venison Taco Soup –

- 2 lbs deer burger
- 1 can V-8 juice
- 2 cans dark kidney beans (do not drain)
- 1 can corn (do not drain)
- 1 package taco mix
- 2 tablespoon onion powder
- 1 tablespoon garlic powder
- 1 tablespoon Tabasco

Cook and drain deer meat in a large pan. Put all ingredients and cook on low for 8 hours (simmer). Serve over corn chips with diced onion and top with cheese.

Shaena's Ham, Venison and Bean soup –

- 1 lb deer burger
- 1 pound diced ham
- 1 large diced yellow onion
- 1 pound bacon, cooked and diced
- 1 tablespoon sugar
- 1 tablespoon pepper
- 1 tablespoon garlic powder
- 1 tablespoon Worcestershire sauce
- 2 cans pinto beans (drained)
- 1 package frozen vegetables
- 1 can V-8 juice

Combine all ingredients in a large crock-pot. Cook on high for six hours. Stirring often.

Serve with corn bread.

Did you know that for centuries, man has harvested all types of deer for venison? It was considered a delicacy by people in medieval times, and large plots of land were used by royalty for hunting deer.

It was also a feast for kings during the Victorian era. Until about 200 years ago, venison had been as important to Thanksgiving dinner as turkey.

Today, no chemicals (steroids, etc.) are used in the deer to make them grow unnaturally, so venison is just as healthy as when they were first harvested 500,000 years ago by early man.

Venison is truly meat fit for Kings.

Buck Trail Chili –

- 5 lbs of deer burger
- 1 pound bacon
- 2 cups red wine
- 2 teaspoons Angostura Bitters
- 4 tablespoons Cumin (ground)
- 4 tablespoons Tabasco sauce
- 4 garlic cloves (minced)
- 2 ½ cups Tomato sauce
- 1 cup tomato paste
- 2 ½ cups chopped stewed tomatoes
- 4 Jalapeno peppers (minced)
- 2 large yellow onions (chopped)
- 1 cup mushrooms (chopped)
- 2 tablespoons dried red pepper flakes
- ½ tablespoon allspice
- 3 tablespoons dried crushed anchos
- ½ teaspoon salt
- 1 shot whiskey

Fry bacon in a large, heavy pot. Remove bacon when done and set aside. Add deer burger, chopped onions, the minced garlic and salt to bacon grease.

Fry the deer burger until done and remove from the pot. Drain off the grease, add wine, tomato sauce, and the bacon which has been crumbled.

Bring wine to boil, add Jalapenos, deer burger, Tabasco sauce, 3 tablespoons cumin, the allspice and whiskey.

Cook for 3 minutes, add tomato paste and cook for 1 ½ hours. Stir often. Add the remaining cumin.
Cook for 15 minutes more and serve with bread and butter.

John's Venison Hash –

- 5 tablespoons bacon drippings
- 1 large yellow onion (chopped)
- 5 lbs chopped venison roast
- 8 medium potatoes (diced)
- 4 tablespoons flour
- 2 cloves minced garlic
- 5 cups beef broth
- 1 tablespoon pepper
- 1 tablespoon seasoned salt
- ½ tablespoon chili powder

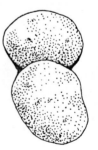

Brown onion and potatoes in the bacon fat. Add flour and brown. Add broth and other ingredients. Let simmer until tender.

Barbecued Beans and Venison –

- 2 lbs deer burger
- 1 garlic clove
- ½ cup ketchup
- ½ cup packed brown sugar
- 15 ounce garbonzo beans
- 16 ounce kidney beans
- 28 ounce baked beans
- 1 large yellow onion
- ½ cup BBQ sauce
- ¼ cup molasses
- 32 ounce great northern beans
- 16 ounce green beans
- 17 ounce pinto beans

In a skillet, brown deer burger with onion and garlic until meat is no longer pink. Drain. Add to your crock-pot with the rest of the ingredients. Cook on high setting for 5 ½ hours.

The hunting gang was getting ready for our annual weeklong deer camp. We all appointed Bubba to get the supplies. Bubba went to town and bought 8 bottles of whiskey, 10 cases of beer and a package of hotdogs.

When he returned back to camp the boys looked in his truck and Billy asked, "Bubba, what are we gonna do with all them hotdogs?"

Deer Spaghetti Sauce –

- 2 lbs deer burger
- 1 ½ cups chopped celery
- 1 garlic clove
- 2 cans tomato soup
- 6 ounces tomato paste
- 12 ounces chili sauce
- ½ tablespoon hot pepper sauce
- 2 tablespoons steak sauce
- 2 tablespoons salt
- 2 tablespoons tyme
- 2 table spoons sage

- 1 green pepper
- 2 cups chopped onion
- ½ cup chopped carrots
- 16 ounces diced tomatoes with liquid
- 1 ½ cups water
- 1 tablespoon Worcestershire sauce
- 2 table spoons sugar
- 2 bay leafs
- 1 tablespoon all spice
- 1 tablespoon olive oil

Add all ingredients to the crock-pot. Cook on high heat for 5 ½ hours. Serve with cooked spaghetti or elbow macaroni. Serve with Texas garlic toast.

Deer Soup Stock –

- 2 large deer bones, cracked
- 1/8 tablespoon nutmeg
- 1/16 tablespoon mace
- 12 peppercorns, crushed
- 8 cups water
- ¼ tablespoon smoked salt

Crack bones after removing from meat (large ham bone). Place in a large pot, add seasonings. Bring to boil, then cover and simmer for three hours.

Strain stock through a tea strainer, then through cloth to remove any particles.

Allow to cool, then skim off any fat, which accumulates. Use as base for soup or stew.

Bubba and Bud took to the woods deer hunting one Iowa fall day. Unbeknownst to Bubba, Bud put on a deer suit, complete with antlers. Bubba mistook him for a deer and shot him.

Bubba took his wounded companion to the hospital. After filling out a few forms he waited. Finally, after several hours, the doctor came out of surgery with bleak news. "There was a chance we could have saved him," the doctor said, "if only you hadn't gutted him too!

Buck Eve Chili –

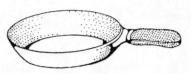

- 6 pound venison roast
- 2 cups beer
- ½ cup Coca-Cola
- 4 chopped yellow onions
- 5 minced garlic cloves
- 2 cups tomato sauce
- 1 cup sour mash whiskey
- 1 cup chopped green peppers
- 1 cup chopped red peppers
- 8 diced green jalapenos peppers
- 2 tablespoon salt
- 3 tablespoon Tabasco sauce
- 1 ½ cup tomato paste
- 1 tablespoon cayenne flakes
- 1 tablespoon all spice
- 4 tablespoon fresh ground
- 2 tablespoon cilantro fresh chopped
- 2 tablespoon peanut oil

Cut meat into ¼ " cubes. Put peanut oil into a large cast iron pot, and heat on medium high, add onions, garlic, meat cubes, and 1 tablespoon of cumin.

Cook until meat is browned. Add tomato sauce, beer, and whiskey, Coca-Cola, peppers, spices and cook on low heat for 45 minutes, covered, stirring often.

Uncover and cook for 20 minutes more. Stir in the remaining cumin and serve.

A good deer hunter would never hit a deer with his truck...deliberately.

Chuck Wagon Venison Soup –

- 1 pound venison; cut into bite- sized pieces
- 1 46 oz can of V-8 juice
- 1 28 oz can of whole tomatoes; undrained and chopped
- 2 large chopped red onions
- 2 tablespoons of Worcestershire sauce
- 1 tablespoon hot sauce
- 4 large peeled and diced potatoes
- 4 medium sliced carrots
- 4 sliced yellow squash
- 3 stalks thinly sliced celery
- 2 green peppers cut in 1 inch pieces

Combine first 6 ingredients in an 8 – quart Dutch oven; bring to a boil. Reduce to medium heat; cover and cook 30 minutes, stirring occasionally.

Stir in potatoes and carrots; cover and cook 20 minutes.

Add remaining vegetables to soup; cook, uncovered, 10 additional minutes or until vegetables are tender. Serve with hard rolls.

Flat Head went deer hunting with two experienced deer hunters, Billy and Bubba. Billy says that he would go first. He leaves the cabin and goes out deer hunting. He's back in an hour with a 10 point buck.

Flat Head says, "How did you do that?" Billy reply's, "Simple, I found tracks, then I followed them and, Wham!, I shot a Buck."

Bubba goes out and does the same thing Billy did. When he comes back with a 10 pointer, Flat Head is astonished and asks the same question,

"How did you do that?" So Bubba says,

"Simple, I found tracks then followed them and then, Wham!, I shot a buck."

"Oh I get it," says Flat Head.

So Flat Head takes his turn in the woods. He doesn't return. When they search for him, Billy and Bubba find him at the hospital. They asked him what happened.

Flat Head says, "I found the tracks and I followed them and, Wham!, The train hit me!

Venison Steaks

Save your Angus for your mother-in-law, I will take a venison steak over Angus anytime.

Boy's there ain't nothing better than a well seasoned, medium rare deer steak grilled over the fire or the coals. Man, if that ain't eating I don't know what is.

Again, I have put together some of my favorite steak recipes for your enjoyment. Note! Make sure to check out the marinades section of this book for even more robust flavors.

Brandied Venison Tenderloin Steaks	48
Creamed Venison Steak	49
Dad's Mustard Fried Venison Steak	51
Deer Lounge Venison Steaks With Scotch Sour Sauce	60
Grilled Venison Tenderloin Steaks	46
Hawkeye Venison Pepper Steak	59
Hunters Choice Venison Tenderloin Steaks	46
No Time Grilled Venison Steak	48
Richard's Venison Steaks With Mushroom Game Sauce	66
Salisbury Steak Venison Style	61
The Duke's Venison Tenderloin Appetizers	51
Venison Hawaiian Style Steak	63
Venison Steak And Gravy	62
Venison Steaks In Wine	56
Venison Steaks Sandwiches	65
Venison Steaks With Chestnuts & Figs	53
Venison Steak With Roquefort	57
Venison Swiss Steak	58
Venison Tenderloin Of The Peppercorn	65

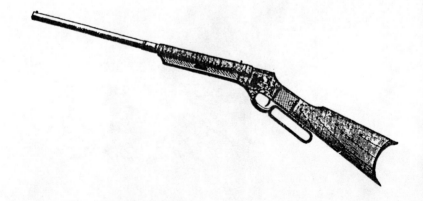

Grilled Venison Tenderloin Steaks

- 2 loin steaks ¾ " thick
- 5 tablespoons butter
- salt and pepper

Coat the top half of each steak with butter, salt and pepper. Grill steaks on greased rack 4 inches above coals for 3 – 6 minutes. Turn steaks, coat top of each steak again with butter, salt and pepper. Grill for 3 – 6 minutes longer.

Hunters Choice Venison Tenderloin Steaks –

- 6 loin steaks ¼ inch thick
- ½ cup seasoned flour
- salt and pepper
- olive oil

Roll each steak in flour until coated, add salt and pepper. Cover the bottom of a large fry pan with the olive oil. Fry steaks on medium heat until nicely brown, turn and fry until juices are clear.

Turn steaks again from time to time to make sure they are tender and mild.

Bubba takes his wife out deer hunting for the first time. It's early in the morning and Bubba is explaining the rules to his wife,

"Now, remember these woods have a lot of greedy people in them, so if you shoot a deer, run right over to it and guard it. If you don't, someone else will take your deer away." The wife nods okay. "Now, this is what we're going to do. See that ridge to your right? You're going to sit on top of that one, and I will sit on this one to the left.

They agree and go to their separate ways. About thirty minutes after sunrise, Bubba hears a gunshot come from the ridge his wife is sitting on. He thinks to himself,

"Cool, her first time out deer hunting and she gets one!" Five more minutes pass, and he hears three gun shots come from the other ridge. He thinks, "Oh great. Now she's in trouble." Being the good husband he was, he ran over to the other ridge. As he reached the top, he came into a clearing where his wife was holding off another man with her gun.

The man is pleading with the wife, saying, "Okay, lady, he's a deer, and he's yours, just let me get my saddle off."

Brandied Venison Tenderloin Steaks –

- 4 loin steaks cut ¾ inch thick
- 4 tablespoons butter
- 3 tablespoons brandy
- 1 tablespoon Worcestershire sauce
- 2 tablespoons garlic powder

Melt butter over medium heat in a large fry pan and quickly sear steaks. Reduce heat and cook for an additional 2 – 6 minutes on each side. Mix the brandy and Worcestershire sauce with the garlic powder and pour over steaks.

Simmer on low heat for 1-2 minutes.

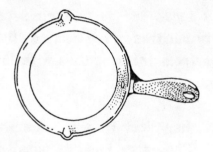

No Time Grilled Venison Steak –

- 4 venison steaks cut ¾ inch thick
- ½ cup apple vinegar
- ½ cup olive oil
- ½ cup Italian dressing

Mix all ingredients together and Marinate steaks for 6 hours.

Grill for 40 minutes or until done to taste, Salt and pepper.

A good deer hunter would never fill his tag on the golf course.

Creamed Venison Steak –

- 4 venison round steaks cut into 2 inch strips
- 6 tablespoons butter
- 3 cans cream of mushroom soup
- 2 teaspoons Celery salt
- ½ tablespoon pepper
- 3 tablespoons chopped parsley
- 4 tablespoons Worcestershire sauce
- 1 tablespoon garlic powder
- ¼ cup pickle relish

(TOPPINGS)

- 1 cup bread crumbs
- 3 tablespoons butter

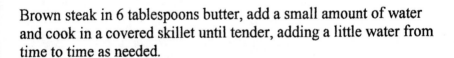

Brown steak in 6 tablespoons butter, add a small amount of water and cook in a covered skillet until tender, adding a little water from time to time as needed.

When done add soup (without water), seasonings, parsley and pickle relish. Put mixture in a greased casserole pan. Sprinkle top with breadcrumbs and dot with butter.

Bake in oven at 350 degrees until breadcrumbs are browned.

My buck was so big...Top ten list...

1. To fit the rack in my trailer, I had to move into a triple-wide.
2. Before I shot this buck, I noticed his hindquarters leaving the ground whenever he dropped his head to feed.
3. My taxidermist charged me by the pound.
4. When I first found this buck's rub, I thought someone had started a clear-cut.
5. The rack looks so lethal; I needed a permit to bring it home.
6. Whenever I show someone the photo of my deer, and, me, they want to know who the kid with the beard is.
7. Even though I was sitting in a tree stand, it was a level shot.
8. Rather than hang the mount on a wall, I have to display it in a reinforced floor console.
9. When I brought the deer home, the ceramic buck in my front yard ran away.
10. If I removed all the velvet off the antlers this size, I could make seat covers for my truck.

DAD'S MUSTARD FRIED VENISON STEAK –

- 6 loin steaks ¾ inch thick
- ¼ teaspoon garlic powder, ¼ teaspoon season salt, ¼ teaspoon pepper and mix together. This is your dry seasoning.
- 4 tablespoons Dijon mustard
- 2 teaspoons horseradish
- 1 ½ cup olive oil

Season steaks with the seasonings. Combine mustard and horseradish. Spread mixture on each side of steaks so that the steaks are fully covered on both sides. Fry in hot olive oil.

Poke with fork and as soon as juices run clear, steaks are done.

Serve with green salad and baked potato.

The Duke's Venison Tenderloin Appetizers –

- 1 two pound loin
- ½ cup red wine
- 3 tablespoons olive oil
- 2 tablespoons Worcestershire sauce
- 1 teaspoon dried thyme
- 1 teaspoon onion powder

- 1 teaspoon cumin seeds
- 1 teaspoon pepper
- ½ teaspoon ground cloves
- 1 teaspoon garlic powder
- ½ teaspoon sugar

Place tenderloin in a shallow dish. Combine wine, oil, and Worcestershire sauce; mix well. Add thyme and remaining ingredients, mixing well. Pour over tenderloin, and cover tightly.

Refrigerate for 8 hours, turning meat occasionally. Remove tenderloin, reserving marinade. Place on rack in roasting pan; insert meat thermometer. Bake at 425 degrees for 30 minutes or until thermometer registers 160 degrees, basting occasionally with marinade.

Allow meat to stand for 10 minutes. Slice into very thin slices. Serve with party rolls, mustard, and mayonnaise.

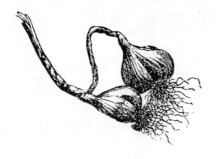

A good deer hunter would never watch the game warden through his scope.

Venison Steaks with Chestnuts & Figs –

- 2 tablespoons butter
- 1 cup chopped green onions
- 1 cup port wine
- 1 ½ cups beef stock (broth)
- 30 peeled chestnuts
- 8 venison medallions
- 4 figs

Melt 1 tablespoon of butter in a heavy saucepan, add a good grinding of black pepper and gently cook the chopped onions. Add the port wine and reduce. Add the stock and the chestnuts and simmer for about 20 minutes or until the sauce becomes syrupy.

Set aside and keep warm. In a heavy frying pan, add a tablespoon of butter. When it is very hot, cook the Venison, searing them for at least one minute on each side, to ensure they are still rare. Meanwhile, butter a baking tray and slice onto it the 4 figs. Place under a grill to heat through.

Divide the sauce and chestnuts between the four heated plates and add to each plate 2 medallions of venison and one of the fig slices. Note- Serve while meat is still warm.

25 Things you'd never hear a deer hunter say

1. " Sorry boy's, I cant go hunting this weekend, my wife wants to snuggle."
2. " Do you think that this blaze orange brings out the color of my eyes?"
3. " Hey guys, I would appreciate it if you didn't smoke or drink at camp."
4. " Who borrowed my Kenny G tape?"
5. " Four- wheel drive is over rated."
6. " Awa man, I broke a nail."
7. " I shot three times at a huge buck and never hit him once."
8. " We're outta beer."
9. " Hey look, a yard sale! Pull over, we can hunt anytime!"
10. " Bullets are too expensive to shoot at paper before the season."
11. " Ted Nugent sucks."
12. " WCW and WWF are fake!"
13. " May I see your low fat menu please."

14. " My cats breath smells like cat food."
15. " Bubba those bibs look a little tight. I hope they feel alright in the crotch."
16. " Dang! There's a run in my coveralls."
17. " Hey boy's I feel like going to Wal-Mart today."
18. " Jeez whiz Flathead your hair smells so pretty."
19. " This snow is just murder on my chapped hands."
20. " Darren roll down the window, I ate chili last night and I just cut one."
21. " I don't want no stinking quad-runner! I like to drag my deer out."
22. " Billy, you got a burger hanging from your nose. I'll get it."
23. " It's too cold for beer, I want hot cocoa."
24. " I was on a four-wheeler when I shot him."
25. " This bow makes my arms hurt when I pull it back."

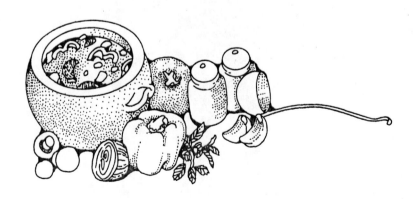

Venison steaks In Wine –

- 4 small venison steaks
- 2 tablespoons butter
- 1 tablespoon fennel
- 1 tablespoon garlic salt
- 1 tablespoon basil
- 1 cup white cooking wine
- 1 tablespoon pepper

In a large frying pan melt butter over medium heat. Put steaks in pan and add fennel, garlic salt, pepper and basil.

Cook venison until meat is tender on both sides. When meat is done remove from pan and sit aside. Add the wine to the pan and simmer for one minute.

Add the steak back to the pan and simmer for 3 minutes. Serve with hash browns.

Venison Steak With Roquefort –

- 1 large venison steak, at least 1 inch thick
- ½ cup butter
- ½ cup Roquefort cheese
- ½ tablespoon garlic powder
- ½ tablespoon Worcestershire sauce

Cream together the butter and cheese. Add garlic and Worcestershire sauce to cheese mixture. Salt and pepper to taste. Place steak on grill racks about six inches above coals. Grill about 15 minutes; turn. Spread the top of the steaks with the cheese mixture and grill for 15 minutes longer. Serve with baked potatoes.

Venison Swiss Steak –

- 2 lbs Venison round steak cut 1 inch thick
- 3 large yellow onions
- 1 ½ cup tomatoes
- 1 cup flour
- 2 tablespoons Worcestershire sauce
- 1 tablespoon garlic salt

Roll the venison steak in flour and beat it with a meat hammer or tenderizer, you really have to pound it in. Season with garlic salt, Worcestershire sauce and pepper. Brown both sides slowly in a heavy skillet, add the tomatoes and onions (sliced).

Cover tightly and cook slowly. Remove from heat when done and thicken the gravy. Serve with mashed potatoes.

Hawkeye Venison Pepper Steak –

- 2 lbs venison round steak
- ½ cup flour
- ½ teaspoon salt
- ½ teaspoon pepper
- 1 large yellow onion, sliced
- 6 ounces of sliced mushrooms
- 3 tablespoons Worcestershire sauce
- 1 sliced green pepper
- 1 cup water
- olive oil

Cut the steaks into 1-inch strips. Coat strips a mixture of flour, salt and pepper. Heat olive oil over medium heat in a large frying pan and lightly brown the meat.

Drain the excess oil. Add the onion, mushrooms, green pepper and Worcestershire sauce.

Stir-fry for 10 minutes add the water, cover and simmer for 30 more minutes. Serve with rice.

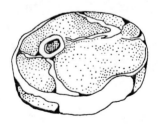

Deer Lounge Venison Steaks with Scotch Sour Sauce

- 2 tablespoons butter
- 1 cup chopped shallots
- 8 cranberries, crushed
- ¼ cup scotch
- ¾ cup orange juice
- 3 tablespoons lemon juice
- 2 tablespoons red currant jelly
- 2 tablespoons Dijon mustard
- 2 teaspoons cornstarch
- 2 tablespoons water
- 1 tablespoon garlic powder
- 1 tablespoon onion powder
- 4 venison porterhouse steaks

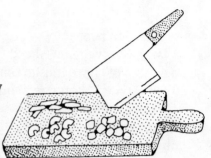

Combine 1-tablespoon butter, shallots and berries in a 2-cup glass measure. Cover with vented plastic wrap. Microwave on high for two minutes.

Add Scotch and microwave on high for one minute. Stir in orange juice, lemon juice, jelly and mustard. Microwave on high for two minutes. Combine cornstarch with water, garlic powder and onion powder. Stir into sauce; microwave on high for one minute and set aside.

Preheat a microwave-browning dish. Rub remaining butter over surface. Immediately, press venison onto hot surface. When brown, turn over. Microwave on high for two minutes. Serve with sauce.

A good deer hunter would never take a beer to a job interview:

Salisbury Steak Venison Style –

- 4 venison steaks (tenderized)
- 2 large yellow onions, cut into thin, long strips
- 2 cans of whole peeled tomatoes
- ¼ cup olive oil
- 1 teaspoon garlic powder
- 1 teaspoon celery salt
- 4 tablespoons Worcestershire sauce

Heat oil in a large saucepan and brown steaks on both sides. Add the remaining ingredients. Cover, turn heat to medium-low and simmer for 45 minutes. Serve with noodles.

Venison Steak and Gravy –

- 3 lbs of venison cube steak
- 1 large yellow onion
- 3 packages of brown gravy mix

In a large skillet, brown the cube steak. After browning, arrange the steaks in a 13 x 9x 2 inch backing pan. Chop the onion and add it to the steak gravy according to the package directions. Pour the gravy over the onion.

Cover with foil and bake at 400 degrees for 1 hour. Serve with hash browns.

Venison Hawaiian Style Steak –

- 3 lbs for thin sliced venison round steak
- ½ stick of unsalted butter
- ½ can of pineapple chunks, No syrup
- 1 head of green cabbage, chopped
- 1 head of purple cabbage, chopped
- 1 bunch of celery, diced
- 3 batches of green onion, sliced
- Soy Sauce

Melt butter in a large skillet. Cook steak in the butter until it is brown. Add veggies and pineapples. Cook uncovered until they are tender. Add the soy sauce and salt and pepper to taste. Serve with rice.

Bubba and D.C. are out deer hunting. Bubba says,

"Did you see that?" D.C. says,

"No."

"A pheasant just flew over head."

"Oh." A couple of minutes later, Bubba says, "Did you see that?"

"No." "There was a 8 pointer walking in the cedars on that hill over there." "Oh." A few minutes later Bubba says,

"Did you see that?" D.C., getting aggravated, says, "Yes I did!" Bubba says, "Then why did you step in it?"

Venison steak sandwiches –

- 2 venison round steaks, cut into thin strips
- 1 can of beef broth
- 1 teaspoon of minced garlic
- smoked cheese slices

In a skillet, heat beef broth and minced garlic to a low boil. Add venison and cook until meat is no longer pink. Serve on brat bun with smoked cheese.

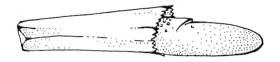

Venison Tenderloin of the Peppercorn –

- 4 gloves of minced garlic
- 1 venison loin
- 3 tablespoons coarsely crushed whole peppercorns
- 2 tablespoons butter
- 1 tablespoon of seasoning salt

Spread garlic over the venison loin and then roll the loin in the peppercorn. Put the loin in a preheated oven at 425 degrees and bake for 15 minutes. Then dot the loin with butter and continue baking for 20 more minutes. Let the tenderloin stand for 5 minutes before slicing.

A good deer hunter will have more pet names for his dog than for his girlfriend.

Richard's Venison Steaks with Mushroom Game Sauce –

- 4 venison steaks cut from the loin
- ground Juniper berries
- 3 tablespoons salt
- ½ cup melted butter
- 2 cups wild mushroom game sauce

Sauce-

- 1 once dried boletus edulis mushrooms
- 2 cups water
- 1 white onion chopped
- 3 tablespoons melted butter
- 4 tablespoons all purpose flour
- 1 cup beef broth
- ½ cup dry red wine
- 6 juniper berries, crushed
- 6 allspice berries, crushed
- 2 tablespoons Dijon mustard
- ½ teaspoon paprika
- 3 ounces of diced dill pickles

Pound the steaks to about ½ inch in thickness. Sprinkle lightly with the juniper berries and salt. Sauté the steaks in butter for about 4 minutes on each side. Heat the wild mushroom game salt and pour over the steaks.
Sauce:

Put the mushrooms in 3 cups of water in a saucepan and bring to a boil, Then reduce the heat and let simmer for 40 minutes.

Remove the reconstituted mushrooms from the broth, and set aside. Sauté the onions in butter until they are tender and add the flour, stir for 1 minute.

Add the simmered mushroom extract, strained meat stock and red wine to the roux mixture, stir until blended and slightly thickened. Add juniper berries, allspice, mustard, paprika, mushrooms and dill pickles. Simmer for 4 minutes. Pour sauce over steaks and serve with wild rice.

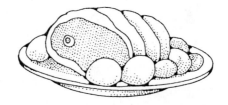

Deer Jerky

You can dog a man's truck. You can laugh at his gun. You can say his dog is stupid and lazy. **But you don't say a damn thing bad about his Jerky without a fight.**

That's one of the first lessons to be learned in the world of deer hunters. A man takes a little more pride when it comes to his jerky making.

Ladies, let's get one thing perfectly clear, when a man makes jerky, there's going to be a mess. So you need to take a breather and go to the mall or whatever ladies do when football is on. Cause a man's got to have some room to create the succulent morsels known as deer jerky.

When it comes right down to it, jerky is probably the number one Favorite meat flavor from venison. I have put together a large

assortment of my favorite jerky recipes. I want to show you the many different ways to prepare jerky. I have listed recipes that will take you from the smoker to the dehydrator, so please study each and every one because they may seem similar but they are indeed different in process and flavor.

Here are a few tips to help you get started:

Always keep your venison roast or steaks about ½ frozen before cutting the thin slices needed for jerky **meat and always have the meat trimmed of fat because fat will allow meat to go rancid.** And most of all don't be afraid to experiment with flavors such as Garlic salt, pizza seasoning, lemon pepper, crushed red pepper, chili powder, smoked salt, liquid smoke, pineapple juice and onion powder are just a few.

Another good tip is to remember to store your jerky in an airtight container or zip lock bags. Storage time on jerky is about 3 weeks at room temperature, 16 weeks in the refrigerator and 30 weeks in the freezer.

Brined Jerky	72
Dry Rub Jerky	81
Grand Pappy's Deer Jerky	74
Mountain Man Soft Jerky	80
My First Jerky	79
Onion Ground Venison Jerky	75
Rick's Blend Jerky	73
Right - A - Way - Ranch Jerky Meat	82
Rodeo Bill's Barbecued Jerky	77
Swamp Witch Microwave Jerky	78

Brined Jerky –

- 5 lbs lean venison
- 1 cup curing salt
- ½ molasses or brown sugar
- 1 teaspoon liquid garlic
- 5 tablespoons black pepper
- 2 quarts water
- onion salt
- garlic powder

Remove all fat and membrane from the meat. Combine the rest of the ingredients. Soak the meat in the solution for 10 hours. Remove the meat and rinse. Pat dry with paper towels. Air-dry for one hour.

Rub in the onion salt, garlic powder and black pepper. Smoke meat for 10 hours or until ready.

Test the meat by twisting a strip of meat. It should be flexible.

Rick's Blend Jerky –

- ½ cup soy sauce
- 4 tablespoons Worcestershire sauce
- 1 teaspoon onion powder
- 1 teaspoon garlic powder
- ¼ teaspoon powdered ginger
- ½ teaspoon Chinese five spice powder
- 2 teaspoons black pepper
- 3 lbs venison roast or steaks

Trim venison completely of fat and cut across grain into slices 1/8 inch thick. To help cut meat thinly, keep about ½ frozen.
Blend all ingredients except meat in a small bowl. Dip each piece of meat into marinade, coating well. Place in shallow dish. Pour remaining marinade over top, cover and refrigerate for 14 hours.

Oven Method: Preheat oven to the lowest setting about 110 degrees. Place several layers of paper towels on baking sheets. Arrange meat in a single layer on prepared sheets and cover with additional toweling. Flatten meat with rolling pin. Discard towels and set meat directly on oven racks. Let dry 8 to 12 hours.

Dehydrator Method: Arrange meat on trays in a single layer and dehydrate 10 to 12 hours, depending on thickness.
Note: Always store jerky in plastic bags or in tightly covered containers in a cool dry place.

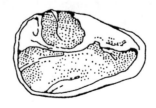

Bud and Bubba are going deer hunting on Bubba's uncle's land. The uncle doesn't want any of his cows getting shot, so he tells them that he has every deer in the area labeled "Deer", so they'll know when they see one.

The next day, the uncle goes out into his front yard and sees his brand new John Deere Tractor dead.

Grand Pappy's Deer Jerky –

- 7 lbs of venison roast
- 1 tablespoon salt
- ¼ tablespoon black pepper
- ¼ teaspoon white pepper
- 1 teaspoon red pepper
- 1 tablespoon meat tenderizer
- 2 tablespoons seasoned salt
- 2 teaspoons Accent
- 1 teaspoon garlic powder
- 1 tablespoon kitchen bouquet
- 2 tablespoons Morton tender quick
- ½ cup Worcestershire sauce
- 1/3 cup soy sauce
- 1/3 cup barbecue sauce
- 1/3/ cup liquid smoke

Cut meat in thin slices. Combine salt, peppers, meat tenderizers, seasoned salt, accent, garlic and onion powders, kitchen bouquet, Morton tender quick, Worcestershire sauce, soy sauce, barbecue sauce and liquid smoke.

Marinate meat in sauce for 24 hours in a sealable plastic bag. Place meat directly on oven racks, line bottom of oven with foil, or rack in a shallow pan and dry in oven for 6 – 8 hours on lowest setting. Continue to dry in a warm oven if needed.

Onion Ground Venison Jerky –

- 2 ounce package of dried onion soup mix
- ¼ cup water
- ¼ cup of soy sauce
- 1 tablespoon of minced garlic
- 1 teaspoon curing salt
- 1 teaspoon liquid smoke
- 2 lbs of lean deer burger

In a bowl, combine onion soup mix and water. Let stand for 10 minutes. Add the remaining ingredients, including the venison, and mix well. Cover and refrigerate for 12 hours.

When done marinating in the refrigerator for 12 hours remove and put through a jerky press, or shape the meat into 2-inch balls. Top it with a mesh sheet. Arrange the meat rounds on the mesh sheets.

Dry at 145 degrees for about 8 hours. With some dehydrators, you may have to turn the rounds to ensure equal drying.

Be sure to blot fat from meatballs with a paper towel from time to time during drying. When jerky is done let stand for 1 hour and then cut thin slices from meatballs.

Last year a group of the boys went deer hunting and paired off in twos for the day. That night, one of the hunters returned back to camp alone, staggering under the weight of an 10 point buck.

"Where's Billy?" asked the other fellows in the camp.

"Billy had a stroke of some kind. He's a couple of miles back up the trail."

"You left Billy laying out there and carried the deer back!? "

A tough call," nodded the hunter, "but I figured no one is going to steal Billy!"

Rodeo Bill's Barbecued Jerky –

- 2 lbs of venison steak or roast
- ½ cup catsup
- ½ cup red wine vinegar
- ¼ cup brown sugar
- 2 teaspoons dry mustard
- 2 teaspoons onion powder
- 2 teaspoons salt
- 1 teaspoon garlic powder
- ½ teaspoon cayenne pepper

Cut meat into ¼ inch thick slices. In a medium bowl combine catsup, vinegar, sugar, mustard, onion powder, salt, garlic powder and cayenne pepper. Stir to dissolve seasonings. Add meat and mix until all surfaces are thoroughly coated. Cover tightly and refrigerate for 12 hours, stirring occasionally. Dry and cure meat in oven or dehydrator.

Swamp Witch Microwave Jerky –

- ½ pound trimmed venison
- ½ teaspoon salt
- ½ teaspoon garlic powder
- 1 teaspoon accent
- ½ teaspoon black pepper
- ¼ cup Worcestershire sauce
- ¼ cup soy sauce
- ¼ cup water
- 8 drops liquid smoke

Cut meat into 1/8-inch thick strips. Combine ingredients in a large bowl. Then place meat with ingredients, in a large zip lock bag making sure meat is totally covered, then place the meat in the refrigerator overnight to marinate. Then place the meat on a microwave roasting rack.

Set the microwave on high for 4 to 6 minutes. After 4 minutes add time in 30-second increments. The purpose is to have dried jerky, which means a color change from brown to dark brown, and a consistency in the meat that has changed from supple to a leathery texture.

My First Jerky –

- 5 lbs 1/8 inch sliced venison
- 4 tablespoons hickory smoked salt
- 2 tablespoons garlic salt
- 2 tablespoons Monosodium glutamate
- 4 tablespoons seasoned pepper
- 1 cup soy sauce
- ½ cup Worcester sauce
- 1 teaspoon accent

Mix all dry ingredients together while oven is warming to 200 degrees. Sprinkle meat with the dry mixture on both sides. Drape meat on oven racks. Place the oven racks in oven with door open 2 inches.

After one hour, baste with mixed sauces, repeating every ½ hour for about 2 hours. Then drop oven heat to 170 degrees and finish meat in about 1-½ hours.

A Good deer hunter will never allow his dog to eat at the table, no matter how good the dog's manners are.

Mountain Man Soft Jerky –

- 10 lbs lean deer burger
- 2/3 cup curing sugar
- 1 teaspoon cardamom
- 1 teaspoon marjoram
- 1 tablespoon MSG
- 1 tablespoon cayenne pepper
- 2 tablespoon black pepper
- 4 tablespoon liquid smoke
- 2 tablespoon water
- 1 teaspoon garlic powder

Mix the spices thoroughly and then add the spices a bit at a time while kneading the meat like dough. Put the meat in the fridge for 8 hours to allow the spices to work through the meat.

After the 8-hour wait, roll the meat out to a 1/8-inch thickness between two pieces of wax paper. Remove the top paper and score the meat into strips and place them in the freezer for about an hour.

Remove the meat and break at the score marks. Place the jerky on wire racks and place them in a 150-degree oven, leaving the door open about two inches.

Turn the jerky once or twice during drying and rotate the racks if the jerky is near the elements and begins to dry to fast. Dry for about 4 hours or until jerky reaches the tenderness you like.

Dry Rub Jerky –

- 3 lbs of lean venison roast
- 3 tablespoons Morton Tender Quick Mix
- 3 tablespoons sugar
- 2 tablespoons black pepper
- 2 tablespoons garlic powder

Cut meat into ¼ inch thick slices, about 1-½ inches wide. Mix together the curing salt and seasoning. Rub all the surfaces of the meat strips with the salt mix.

Place meat in a zip lock bag and refrigerate for two hours. Rinse the cured meat under running water and pat dry with a paper towels.

Arrange on drying rack or oven rack and dry at 150 degrees for about 3 to 4 hours.

Right-A-Way-Ranch Jerky Meat –

- 4 lbs of lean venison roast or loins
- 1 can cola (not diet)
- 10 ounces Worcestershire sauce
- 10 ounces teriyaki sauce
- 3 tablespoons liquid smoke
- 4 tablespoons black ground pepper
- 3 tablespoons brown sugar
- 1 tablespoon garlic powder

Cut meat into ¼ inch thick slices. Combine all ingredients. Place meat and ingredients into plastic zip lock bags and marinate meat overnight. Place meat in smoker and smoke according to smoker instructions. Or Use the dehydrator or oven methods.

Venison Marinades

When it comes right down to it, marinades and sauces are about the number one taste factor that truly enhances the great flavor of venison.

Marinades serve two different functions; as a tenderizer and as a flavor enhancer. As most of you probably already know that some tough cuts of venison benefit a great deal from the tenderizing effects of marinating.

Marinating is like matchmaking. The goal is a harmonious union, a marriage of distinctive yet complementary qualities. And even with a good marinade bringing out the best of these qualities in venison takes a little time.

Grilled and smoked venison meats all take on a more appealing taste, texture and appearance when they have been marinated.

Marinating times depend on the type of cooking you will be doing. I recommend that all venison meat at least marinate four to eight hours. Always marinate in the refrigerator.

Billy's Beer And Deer Marinade	92
Bubba's Deer Sauce	93
Bubba's Old Time Deer Marinade	.86
Creole Venison Roast Marinade Smoker Style	.90
Darren's Venison Steak And Wine Marinade	90
Flat Head's Red Neck All Purpose Bourbon Marinade	.91
Jack Daniel's Deer Marinade	.94
Jimmy's Old Buck Marinade	.95

The Deer Hunt

1:00 am Alarm clock rings
2:00 am Hunting partners arrive, drag you out of bed
2:30 am Throw everything except the kitchen sink into the pick-up

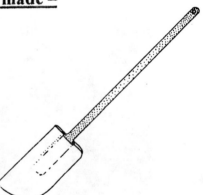

Bubba's Old Time Deer Marinade –

- 1 lemon (squeezed for juice)
- ½ cup apple vinegar
- ¼ tarragon
- 2 sliced onions
- 1 teaspoon chili powder
- ½ cup water
- 1 tablespoon salt
- 2 bay leaves
- 1 tablespoon black pepper
- ½ cup tomato catsup
- 1 crushed garlic clove

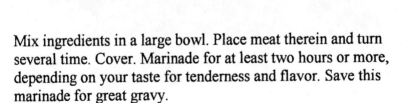

Mix ingredients in a large bowl. Place meat therein and turn several time. Cover. Marinade for at least two hours or more, depending on your taste for tenderness and flavor. Save this marinade for great gravy.

3:00 am Leave for the deep woods
3:15 am Back home to pick up gun
3:30 am Set up camp. Forgot the damn tent, go back home
4:00 am Drive like hell to get to the woods before daylight
4:30 am Set up camp
6:05 am Head for the woods
6:06 am See six deer
6:07 am Take aim and squeeze trigger

6:08 am CLICK
8:00 am Load gun while watching deer go over the hill
9:00 am Head back to camp
12:00 NOON Fire gun for help-eat wild berries
12:15 PM Run out of bullets - six deer come back
12:20 p.m. Strange feeling in stomach
12:30 p.m. Realize you ate poison berries
12:45 p.m. Rescued
12:55 p.m. Rushed to hospital to have stomach pumped
3:00 p.m. Arrive back at camp
3:30 p.m. Leave camp to kill deer
4:00 p.m. Return to camp for bullets

4:01 p.m. Load gun - leave camp again
5:00 p.m. Empty gun on squirrel that is bugging you
6:00 p.m. Arrive at camp - see deer grazing in camp
6:01 p.m. Load gun
6:02 p.m. Fire gun

6:03 p.m. One dead pick-up
6:05 p.m. Hunting buddy arrives in camp dragging large buck
6:06 p.m. Repress desire to shoot hunting buddy
6:07 p.m. Fall into camp fire
6:10 p.m. Change clothes - throw burned ones onto fire
6:15 p.m. Take pick-up, leave hunting buddy and his stinking deer in camp
6:25 p.m. Pick-up boils over - shot hole in block
6:26 p.m. Start walking
6:30 p.m. Stumble and fall, drop gun in mud
6:35 p.m. See large 10 point buck
6:37 p.m. Fire gun, blow up barrel - plugged with mud
6:38 p.m. Mess pants
6:40 p.m. Wrap gun around tree
9:00 p.m. Home at last

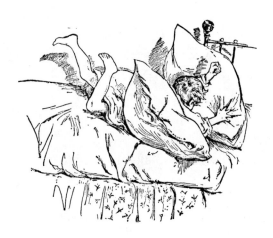

Darren's Venison Steak and Wine Marinade –

- ½ cup ketchup
- ½ cup V-8 juice
- ½ cup red wine
- 1 bay leaf
- 2 tablespoons garlic salt

Mix ingredients in a large bowl add venison steaks. Marinade steaks in refrigerator for 12 hours. (Great for the grille)

Creole Venison Roast Marinade Smoker Style –

- ½ cup oil
- ¼ Wild turkey bourbon
- 2 tablespoon soy sauce
- 2 tablespoons Worcestershire sauce
- 3 tablespoons cayenne pepper
- 1 tablespoon garlic powder
- 1 tablespoon onion powder
- ½ tablespoon coarse ground black pepper

Mix all ingredients well in a large bowel. Add meat and marinate for 12 hours in the refrigerator. Remove meat from marinade. Pad dry with paper towels and place in the smoker.

Flat Head's Red Neck All Purpose Bourbon Marinade

- 2 carrots
- 1 sliced yellow onion
- 1 minced garlic clove
- 2 bay leaves
- 5 sprigs parsley
- 1 ½ tablespoons cracked black peppercorns
- 2 cups white wine
- ½ cup apple vinegar
- 4 cups water
- ¼ cup Wild Turkey Bourbon

Mix all ingredients in a large bowl. Add meat and refrigerate for 8 hours. You can use this for roast, steaks, and tidbits. This will marinate up to six pounds of deer.

Billy's Beer and Deer Marinade –

- 2 cans of beer
- 1 tablespoon of salt
- ½ cup olive oil
- ½ tablespoon cayenne pepper
- 1 tablespoon vinegar
- 1 tablespoon horseradish
- 1 tablespoon onion powder
- 1 tablespoon garlic powder
- 1 tablespoon lemon juice
- 1 bay leaf

Mix all ingredients together. Add deer meat and marinate for 6 hours. Use as a basting sauce for the meat as it cooks.

If a man is talking alone in the timber, with no woman there to hear him, is he still wrong??

Bubba's Deer Sauce –

- 2 peeled and chopped carrots
- 1 chopped yellow onion
- 1 chopped shallot
- 2 tablespoons olive oil
- 2 ½ cups red wine vinegar
- 3 bay leaves
- 3 parsley stalks
- 10 whole juniper berries
- 1 tablespoon salt
- 10 whole peppercorns

Sauté chopped vegetables in the olive oil until lightly brown. Add remaining ingredients and bring to a boil. Reduce heat and simmer for 15 minutes. Make sure sauce is cool before using. Bubba's deer sauce can be refrigerated for about 2 ½ weeks.

Jack Daniel's Deer Marinade –

- ½ cup Jack Daniel's Whiskey
- ½ cup soy sauce
- ½ cup Dijon mustard
- ½ cup minced green onions
- ½ cup brown sugar
- 1 tablespoon salt
- 2 tablespoon Worcestershire sauce
- 2 tablespoons crushed black peppercorns
- 1 tablespoon garlic salt

Mix all ingredients together. Add deer meat and marinate for 8 hours in refrigerator. This marinade is great for broiled or grilled venison steaks, use to baste during cooking.

Jimmy's Old Buck Marinade –

- 1 cup dry white wine
- 1 cup cider vinegar
- ½ cup chopped green onions
- ½ cup orange juice
- ½ cup lemon juice
- ½ cup soy sauce
- 1 tablespoon cayenne pepper
- 1 tablespoon garlic powder
- 1 tablespoon onion powder
- 1 tablespoon brown sugar
- 2 tablespoons black pepper
- 1 tablespoon lemon pepper
- 3 tablespoons all spice
- ½ tea spoon cinnamon
- ½ teaspoon nutmeg
- ½ tablespoon honey
- 1 bay leaf

Combine all ingredients in a large saucepan and bring to boil. After ingredients come to a boil, simmer for 10 minutes then allow the marinade to cool.

After cooling and meat and let stand in refrigerator for 12 hours.

Grille or smoke meat, while basting with sauce.

This is a special sauce made to tenderize and add flavor to a big old white tail buck. However, I love the flavor this sauce brings to all deer meat and I highly recommend you try it often.

Venison Sausage, Casserole's, Roast and other Goodie's

Sausage is known to be the oldest and most enduring form of processed meat. In some respects, it may even be considered the world's very first "convenience food."

The history of sausage production parallels the recorded history of man and civilization. In fact, for as long as man has been carnivorous, the intestinal tract of meat animals has been used for sausage casings.

It's only during the last thousand years, however, that sausage making has come into its own as a venerable and highly developed craft. The practitioners of this trade have fostered a rich tradition. Families have handed down their particular sausage making art

over several generations and across dozens of nations, with each "wurstmacher" contributing his taste and heritage to the art.

The art of sausage making was also influenced by the availability of the various ingredients, which went into the sausage. With venison so readily available, it would be safe to say that the most popular sausage makers used deer meat. Today many deer hunters have sausage made for them by the local meat locker or the meat is sent out to a specialty smokehouse sausage maker.

Smoked venison summer sausage is probably the number one snack or gift among deer hunters during the holiday season. Deer hunters and their families will try several types of sausage and comment on the texture and taste.

In most cases the men will head off to the den or garage to talk about the year's hunt, while the women huddle up and poke fun at us.

D.C."S Venison Summer Sausage..101
Flat Head's Venison Sausage...101
Grandma Barb's Jellied Venison Salad..111
Grandpa Black's Venison German Sausage....................................100
Iowa Roast Of Venison...116
Kenny's Opening Day Breakfast Sausage...104
Jerry's Venison Bologna..107
Old Man Wilke's Venison Sausage Balls..103
Scout's Venison And 4 Beans..107
Stacy's Barbecued Venison Ribs...113
The Duke's Pickled Venison Heart...108
Venison Casserole...109
12 Pointer Deer Loaf...114

Grandpa Black's Venison German Sausage –

- 50 lbs deer burger
- 50 lbs fresh ground pork
- 1 ¾ cup non iodized sack salt
- 3 ounces Morton quick cure
- 3 ounces ground black peppercorn
- 3 ounces minced garlic
- 12 tablespoons sage
- 6 tablespoons apple vinegar
- 12 tablespoon Cayenne pepper

Mix all the ingredients together and add 2 quarts cold water when mixing. Place mixed ingredients in casings. Boil in beer or great for grilling.

Flat Head's Venison Sausage –

- 5 lbs cubed venison
- 1 pound cubed pork suet
- 3 tablespoons salt
- 1 tablespoon black pepper
- 1 teaspoon cayenne pepper
- 1 teaspoon paprika
- 1 teaspoon sage
- 1 tablespoon garlic powder
- Sausage casings

After grinding and mixing the venison and suet with the seasonings, fry a small patty to check for taste. If it is too mild add a small amount of red pepper until proper until proper taste is reached; if it's too hot, add more venison. Stuff in casings and smoke 28 hours.

D.C.'S Venison Summer Sausage –

- 8 lbs deer burger
- 4 lbs ground pork
- 5 tablespoons salt
- 3 tablespoons brown sugar

- 2 tablespoons coriander
- 1 ½ teaspoons cayenne pepper
- 3 tablespoons garlic salt
- 3 tablespoons garlic powder
- 1 teaspoon ground ginger
- 1 teaspoon ground mustard
- 6 teaspoons mustard seed
- 2 teaspoon Morton quick cure

Mix together all meat and seasonings. Stuff meat into casings. Smoke at 100 degrees with heavy smoke for 3 hours, then maintain 100 degrees in smoker for 15 hours.

Raise smoker temp to 165 degrees for three hours to reach 142 internal temp of the sausage. Remove from the smoker and cool in cold water until the sausage reaches room temp. Refrigerate. Serve with cheese and crackers.

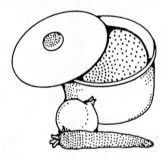

Poor Folk Venison sausage --

- 2 lbs of deer burger
- 1 teaspoon crushed black peppercorn
- 1 teaspoon crushed mustard seed
- 1 teaspoon garlic powder
- 1 teaspoon onion powder

- 2 tablespoons Morton quick tender

Mix all ingredients together and form into two rolls about 2 inch in diameter. Roll in aluminum foil to get the rolls nice and round.

Place in refrigerator for 14 hours. Set oven to 300 degrees. Take sausage and poke several holes in foil bottom with a fork.

Next fill a pan with 2 inches of water and put sausage with holes down in pan. Cook for 1-½ hours. Then bake for one hour in oven with foil off. Rewrap with foil and keep in refrigerator for 3 weeks.

Old Man Wilke's Venison Sausage Balls –

- 2 lbs deer burger
- ½ cup dry breadcrumbs
- 1 egg; beaten
- 1 teaspoons salt
- ½ cup mashed potatoes
- 1 teaspoon brown sugar
- 1 teaspoon pepper
- ½ teaspoon ground all spice
- ½ teaspoon ground nutmeg
- ½ teaspoon ground cloves
- ½ teaspoon ground ginger

Mix all ingredients together and shape into one-inch balls. Brown well in butter, stirring often. Cover and cook over low heat for 20 minutes. Great snack while cleaning deer with the boys.

Kenny's Opening Day Breakfast Sausage --

- 2 lbs deer burger
- 2 lbs ground pork
- 2 tablespoons salt
- 1 tablespoon black pepper
- ½ teaspoon garlic powder
- ½ teaspoon sage
- ½ teaspoon cayenne pepper

Mix all ingredients together and fry in patties. This is a breakfast sausage to eat with eggs and toast while talking about the upcoming hunt.

25 More Things You'd Never hear a Deer Hunter Say

1. " I want a mountain bike instead of a new scope for my rifle."
2. " Pass me the tofu."
3. " Deer season is too long; I should spend more time with my wife."
4. "The tires on my truck are to big."
5. " You can't burn that in a campfire."
6. " I'll show you where I found some fresh buck sign."
7. " Duct tape won't fix that."
8. " I've never got the hang to sharpening a knife."
9. " My truck won't go through that."
10. " How about some poetry reading tonight?"
11. " Let's go shopping, hunting can wait."
12. " Bubba, those jeans make your butt look big, and your belt don't match your boots."
13. " We don't need camp meat, I'll go to the store and buy some."

14. "I took a good picture of a 12 pointer from my tree stand today!"
15. "Honey, you're right I don't need a new gun."
16. "Hey! Lets take our wives to hunting camp with us!"
17. "He's to big to shoot, I won't be able to drag him out."
18. "I'm a vegetarian."
19. "Why don't we take a nice white zinfandel wine to deer camp rather than the regular old beer."
20. "Deer hunting is getting old, Billy."
21. "Man, I can't hit the broadside of a barn."
22. "I have too much camouflage clothing, I'm buying a nice sweater."
23. "Bubba, I think we're lost."
24. "It's too cold to hunt."
25. "What do you mean? I always wear cologne when I hunt."

Jerry's Venison Bologna –

- 5 lbs of deer burger
- ¼ cup Morton quick tender salt
- ½ cup olive oil
- 1 tablespoon garlic salt
- 1 tablespoon hickory salt
- ½ teaspoon onion salt
- 1 tablespoon black pepper
- 1 teaspoon liquid smoke

Mix all ingredients together. Divide and pack into 3 bread pans. Bake for two hours at 300 degrees. Drain off grease while hot. Cool and freeze.

Scout's Venison and 4 beans –

- 2 lbs chunked venison
- 1 pound bacon
- 1 can pork and beans
- 1 can lima beans
- 1 can kidney beans
- 1 can navy beans

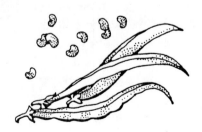

- 1 yellow onion, chopped
- 1 green pepper, chopped
- 1 cup yellow mustard
- 1 cup catsup
- 1 teaspoon brown sugar
- 1 teaspoon salt
- 1 teaspoon black pepper
- 1 teaspoon garlic powder

Brown venison and bacon. Put all ingredients in a crock-pot and cook for four hours on high.

The Duke's Pickled Venison Heart –

- 1 deer heart
- ½ teaspoon brown sugar
- 3 small white onions
- ½ quart cold water
- ½ teaspoon salt
- ½ teaspoon black pepper
- ½ tablespoon garlic salt
- apple vinegar

Set aside 1-quart jar. Boil deer heart in a large pan filled with enough water to cover heart. When water starts to boil add brown sugar and boil until cooked. Drain heart and cool in refrigerator. Dice cooked heart into chunks slice onions in thin slices.

Mix onions and meat and place in quart jar. Add ½ quart of cold water. Put in salt, garlic powder and pepper. Finish filling jar with apple vinegar.

Placed cover on jar, shake and place in refrigerator for 3 days.

Venison Casserole –

- 1 pound deer Burger
- 1 yellow onion, diced
- 1 can cheddar cheese soup
- 1 can cream of celery soup
- 1 bag tatter tots

Brown deer burger with onions, drain and press into a 9x9 pan. Mix the two cans of soup, do not add water. Spread soup over meat. Cover the entire surface with the tatter tots. Bake at 350 degrees for 45 minutes. Salt and pepper to taste.

Deer in Beer –

- 2 pound deer roast
- ¼ teaspoon salt
- ¼ teaspoon black pepper
- 2 cans of your favorite beer
- ½ cup brown sugar
- 2 tablespoon molasses
- 1 tablespoon garlic powder

Place meat in a large bowl and pour beer over it. Cover and marinate in the refrigerator overnight.

Then, remove venison and pat dry, pour beer, sugar, garlic powder and molasses in sauce pan and cook over medium heat, stirring it until sugar dissolves.

Sprinkle the meat with salt and pepper and place in a large pan or Dutch oven, then pour the beer mixture over it.

Cover with a lid and bring to a boil, then reduce heat and simmer for two hours.

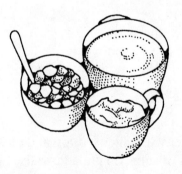

Grandma Barb's Jellied Venison Salad –

- 1 ½ tablespoons unflavored gelatin
- ½ cup cold water
- 1 bouillon cube
- 1 ½ cups boiling water
- ¼ cup vinegar
- ½ teaspoon salt
- 2 cups cooked, diced venison
- 2 tablespoons chopped green pepper
- 2 tablespoons diced pimiento
- 4 chopped sweet pickles
- 2 tablespoon diced celery
- 2 tablespoon diced onion
- 2 tablespoons cooked cut green beans

Soak gelatin in cold water. Dissolve bouillon cube and gelatin in boiling water. Add vinegar and salt. Cool this mixture and when just beginning to set add the rest of the ingredients.

Pour into individual molds or a greased 8-inch square baking dish. Chill and serve on a bed of lettuce with mayonnaise.

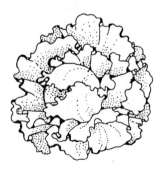

Bubba and Jerry go hunting. Jerry has never gone deer hunting while Bubba has hunted all his life.

When they get to the timber, Bubba tells Jerry to sit by a tree and not make a sound while Bubba checks out a deer stand. After he gets about a quarter of a mile away, Bubba hears a blood – curdling scream.

He rushes back to Jerry and yells, "I thought I told you to be quiet!" Jerry says, "Hey, I tried. I really did. When those snakes crawled over me, I didn't make a sound. When that coyote was breathing down my neck, I didn't make a peep.

But when those two chipmunks crawled up my pants leg and said, "Should we take them with us or eat them here?" I couldn't keep quiet any more!"

Stacy's Barbecued Venison Ribs –

- 4 lbs venison ribs
- 4 tablespoons brown sugar
- 32 ounces tomato sauce
- 4 tablespoons vinegar
- 2 teaspoons yellow mustard
- olive oil

In a roaster arrange ribs. Brush lightly with olive oil and sprinkle with salt and pepper. Bake at 350 degrees until well done, turning once. Pour off juices.

Combine vinegar, brown sugar and mustard with tomato sauce and pour over the ribs.

Bake until done, basting often with the sauce.

12 Pointer Deer Loaf –

- 2 ½ lbs deer burger
- 1 large yellow onion
- 1 bell pepper
- 2 eggs
- 1 cup bread crumbs
- 1 garlic clove
- 3 tablespoons chili powder
- Seasonings, salt and pepper etc…
- 1 can tomato sauce
- 4 strips of bacon

Mix the first 8 ingredients and put in a greased baking dish. Place bacon strips on top of loaf. Pour the tomato sauce over all. Bake at 350 degrees for 1 ½ hours or until done.

Becky's Sausage Muffins –

- ½ pound venison sausage
- 1/3 cup chopped green onions
- 1 six ounce box of Bisquick
- ½ teaspoon dry mustard
- ¼ teaspoon ground red pepper
- ½ cup milk
- ½ cup finely shredded cheddar cheese

In a large skillet, combine sausage and onion. Cook over medium heat until sausage is brown, stirring to make crumbly. Drain well.

Combine Bisquick, mustard, pepper and mix well. Add milk and stir just until moist. Stir in the sausage mixture and cheese. Spoon in the mixture into greased muffin tins.

Bake at 350 degrees for 14 minutes or until the muffins are golden brown. Remove from tins immediately. This meal is great with gravy on top.

Iowa Roast of Venison –

- 4 pound venison roast
- 30 pearl onions
- 1 large chopped yellow onion
- 1 pound chopped fresh mushrooms
- 1 tablespoon tomato sauce
- 2 cups beef stock
- 1 cups dry red wine
- 3 tablespoons flour
- ¼ tablespoon salt
- 2 tablespoons butter
- 1 bay leaf

Coat roast with flour and brown in butter in a large pan with the chopped yellow onion. When roast is completely brown, remove roast and onions and place in a slow cooker. Add the remaining ingredients and slow cook for 8 hours or until meat is done.

The Deer Hunter Temperature Conversion Chart

- 60 above
- Floridians wear coats, gloves and woolly hats.
- Deer hunters sunbathe.

- 50 above
- New Yorkers try to turn on the heat.
- Deer hunters scout out trails.

- 40 above
- Italian cars won't start.
- Deer hunters drive their trucks with the windows down.

- 32 above
- Distilled water freezes.
- Deer hunters build tree stands.

- 20 above
- Californians shiver uncontrollably.
- Deer hunters have the last cookout before it gets cold.

- 15 above
- New York landlords finally turn on the heat.
- Deer hunters throw on a camo sweatshirt.

- 0 degrees
- Californians fly to Mexico.
- Deer hunters lick their gun barrels.

- 20 below
- People in Miami cease to exist.
- Deer hunters get out their winter coats.

- 40 below
- Hollywood disintegrates.
- Deer hunters drink beer and eat chili talking about the upcoming hunt.

- 60 below
- Polar bears begin to evacuate Antarctica.
- Deer hunters postpone growing a beard until it gets cold enough.

- 80 below
- Mt. St. Helen's freezes.
- Deer hunters drink beer and watch hunting videos.

- 100 below
- Santa Claus abandons the North Pole.
- Deer hunters get frustrated when they can't thaw the keg.

- 297 below
- Microbial life survives on dairy products.
- Deer hunter's wives complain of hubby's with cold hands.

- 460 below
- All atomic motion stops.
- Deer hunters start saying " Cold 'nuff for ya?'

- 5oo below
- Hell freezes over.
- Deer hunters let a 12-point buck go because it's 10 minutes after dusk.

10 ways to tell if junior is a deer hunter

1. As a baby, he preferred sucking on a deer grunt tube rather than a pacifier.

2. He dressed up as Ted Nugent for Halloween.

3. When he discovered girls, he started using a cover scent instead of cologne.

4. His school science fair project was entitled " How To Taxidermy Your Game At Home."

5. He put his science fair award on the shelf next to his bullet collection.

6. His subscription to Sports Afield Magazine doesn't run out until 2049.

7. Instead of baseball statistics, he quotes the measurements of top ten scoring Boone and Crockett bucks – both typical and atypical.

8. He does his schoolbook reports on: Whitetail Population Studies and Feed Supplement effects on Antler Development.

9. He ended up in detention because he used his fists to defend his right to wear his favorite t - shirt; which reads " Man didn't get to the top of the food chain by eating vegetables."

10. He'll only go to collage when they come up with a major in " Taking Trophy Bucks."

TEN RULES ON HOW TO ACT AROUND WOMEN HUNTERS

1. If she is has seen game, and you haven't, think about it. She may know something you don't. Beginner's luck really doesn't help much during difficult conditions.

2. Don't let the coy smile fool you. If she has a plan for driving big bucks out of cover, she could do the brush-dogging just as easily as you, but will use all her charms to make sure she'll be the one in the best position to get a shot.

3. When it comes to skinning and butchering her deer, she does like a little help....with sawing the pelvis and lifting the quarters. Indiscriminate and ignorant advice will be ignored.

4. If she forgets some important item, like binoculars; or if you have a new pair to try out, she will be happy to wear your's.

5. She can, and will, field dress and drag her own deer; but if you just happen to be in the area, you can " show her how to do it."

6. If the hunting is bad; really slow, she does not feel the need to leave camp unless the ambiance of the

day demands. (A buck will probably come through camp when she's there anyway.)

7. She does not like to be ignored. If she has a buck hanging, get out your camera and your admiration. (Give her a chance to brush her hair and freshen her camo make-up before taking the picture.)

8. If she's seeing game, and you're not, treat her like one of the guys; ask for help. If she tells you that you are hunting in the wrong area, listen.

9. If you've bagged a buck, and she hasn't seen any deer, offer advice, but never in a condescending way.

10. If this is her first time out, be patient, encourage her. Remember this is hunting, not war.

Be kind and courteous. If you play it right, she may just share her homemade Iced Tea and deer jerky with you.

Tale Tales Of Deer Hunting

Three guys went out hunting and they brought some bottles of whiskey with them.

They were sitting around in the cabin that night by the fire talking. The first guy says, " I'll bet I can go out there in those woods and be back with a buck in half an hour," and they all slapped down a $100 bill and bet he couldn't do it.

Then they drank some more whiskey. The next guy says, " I bet I can go out with just a knife and be back in half an hour with a buck – and they each slapped $200 down to bet he couldn't do it.

They sat for another hour drinking and by now they were all smashed. The third guy says, " I'll bet I can go out there with my bare hands and in a half an hour be back with a 10 point buck."

The other two say, "Fine. Lets see you do it," and they each slap down their money. He gets outside, where there is snow on the ground and its just freezing cold.

The cold air sobers him up a little and he thinks, " What on earth am I doing out here?" and he heads back to the cabin. Just then he hears a big grunt! It's a huge buck. He runs for the cabin and the buck runs after him.

He comes to the door and turns the handle, opens the door, and trips over the welcome mat, falling flat on his face.

The buck is running so fast that he can't stop and he runs right over the guy and on in to the room. The fellow looks up and yells, " Skin this one boy's, I'll be back in a half an hour with the other one."

The Truth About Beer And Deer

Billy and Rick went to the bar one afternoon. Billy was explaining his theory about beer and deer to his buddy Rick. And here's how it went:

"Well, you see Rick; it's like this...a herd of deer can only move as fast as the slowest deer. And when the herd is hunted, it is the slowest and weakest ones at the back that are killed first.

This natural selection is good for the herd as a whole, because the general speed and health of the whole group keeps improving by the regular killing of the weakest members.

In much the same way, the human brain can only operate as fast as the slowest brain cells. Excessive intake of beer, as we all know, kills brain cells, but naturally it attacks the slowest and weakest brain cells first.

In this way, regular consumption of beer eliminates the weaker brain cells, making the brain faster and more efficient. And that's why you always feel smarter after kicking back a few beers."

To Sum It Up

Between a boys first rifle and a tottering old man you can find a peculiar creature that is known as a "Deer Hunter".

We come in all shapes and sizes but we all have the same dream: to rush to the woods when hunting season opens and to enjoy every minute of each hunting trip.

We are found everywhere from trying to walk through the woods in dry leaves, dodging saw briers in thick clear cuts, bogged down in swamps, fighting the cold and rain, fighting the alarm clock at 4:00 A.M. or telling how the big buck got away at work.

Mothers love us, girls don't understand us, wives give up on us, the boss envies us and heaven helps us.

We the "Deer Hunters" are luck with blistered feet and beauty caught in a driving rainstorm with all odds against us. When others are busy thinking of their work the deer hunter is thinking of old logging roads, green fields, swamps and the country side. All we can talk about is the rut, scrapes, guns, ammo and lures to use.

A " Deer Hunter" looks like a bum at times in his old clothes. He eats Vienna sausage from the country store as if it where a steak dinner.

He can sit in a tree stand for hours, but at home last only a few minutes. He has the energy of a hurricane when scouting for big bucks, but hires the neighbors kid to mow and rake the lawn.

He has the courage of a lion and the enthusiasm of a firecracker as he sits in the early morning darkness waiting on first light.

The "Deer Hunter" likes comfortable old clothes, holidays, vacations during hunting season and other hunters. Don't expect him to show up on time for birthdays, anniversaries and reunions. He is not much on kinfolks that visit on weekends, social gatherings, neckties, working overtime on weekends and neighbors that don't hunt.

Who else but a " Deer Hunter" can get things like a compass that doesn't work, two stale sandwiches, a leaky bottle of deer scent and a copy of Out Life all into one hunting coat.

Of all things said of the " Deer Hunter" one thing that you can count on if you only listen long enough, you are sure to hear him say:

Just Wait Till Next Season !!!

Please send me ___ copies at $9.95 each of the *The Venison Cookbook* . Also, add $2.00 shipping and handling for each book. (Make check payable to **QUIXOTE PRESS**.)

Name _____

Street _____

City _____

SEND ORDER TO:
QUIXOTE PRESS
1854-345 Avenue
Wever IA 52658
1-800-571-2665

Since you have enjoyed this book, perhaps you would be interested in some of these others from **QUIXOTE PRESS**.

ARKANSAS BOOKS

ARKANSAS' ROADKILL COOKBOOK
by Bruce Carlson ....paperback $7.95
REVENGE OF ROADKILL
by Bruce Carlson ....paperback $7.95
LET'S US GO DOWN TO THE RIVER 'N...
by Various Authors ....paperback $9.95
TALL TALES OF THE MISSISSIPPI RIVER
by Dan Titus ....paperback $9.95
LOST & BURIED TREASURE OF THE MISSISSIPPI RIVER
by Netha Bell & Gary Scholl ....paperback $9.95
TALES OF HACKETT'S CREEK
by Dan Titus ....paperback $9.95
101 WAYS TO USE A DEAD RIVER FLY
by Bruce Carlson ....paperback $7.95
VACANT LOT, SCHOOL YARD & BACK ALLEY GAMES
by Various Authors ....paperback $9.95
HOW TO TALK MIDWESTERN
by Robert Thomas ....paperback $7.95
ARKANSAS COOKIN'
by Bruce Carlson ....(3x5) paperback $5.95

DAKOTA BOOKS

HOW TO TALK DAKOTA ....paperback $7.95
Some Pretty Tame, but Kinda Funny Stories About Early
DAKOTA LADIES-OF-THE-EVENING
by Bruce Carlson ....paperback $9.95
SOUTH DAKOTA ROADKILL COOKBOOK
by Bruce Carlson ....paperback $7.95

REVENGE OF ROADKILL
by Bruce Carlson ....paperback $7.95
101 WAYS TO USE A DEAD RIVER FLY
by Bruce Carlson ....paperback $7.95
LET'S US GO DOWN TO THE RIVER 'N...
by Various Authors ....paperback $9.95
LOST & BURIED TREASURE OF THE MISSOURI RIVER
by Netha Bell ....paperback $9.95
MAKIN' DO IN SOUTH DAKOTA
by Various Authors ....paperback $9.95
THE DAKOTAS' VANSHING OUTHOUSE
by Bruce Carlson ....paperback $9.95
VACANT LOT, SCHOOL YARD & BACK ALLEY GAMES
by Various Authors ....paperback $9.95
HOW TO TALK MIDWESTERN
by Robert Thomas ....paperback $7.95
DAKOTA COOKIN'
by Bruce Carlson ....(3x5) paperback $5.95

ILLINOIS BOOKS

ILLINOIS COOKIN'
by Bruce Carlson ....(3x5) paperback $5.95
THE VANISHING OUTHOUSE OF ILLINOIS
by Bruce Carlson ....paperback $9.95
A FIELD GUIDE TO ILLINOIS' CRITTERS
by Bruce Carlson ....paperback $7.95
Some Pretty Tame, but Kinda Funny Stories About Early
ILLINOIS LADIES-OF-THE-EVENING
by Bruce Carlson ....paperback $9.95

ILLINOIS' ROADKILL COOKBOOK
by Bruce Carlson ....paperback $7.95
101 WAYS TO USE A DEAD RIVER FLY
by Bruce Carlson ....paperback $7.95
HOW TO TALK ILLINOIS
by Netha Bell ....paperback $7.95
TALL TALES OF THE MISSISSIPPI RIVER
by Dan Titus ....paperback $9.95
TALES OF HACKETT'S CREEK
by Dan Titus ....paperback $9.95
LOST & BURIED TREASURE OF THE MISSISSIPPI RIVER
by Netha Bell & Gary Scholl ....paperback $9.95
STRANGE FOLKS ALONG THE MISSISSIPPI
by Pat Wallace ....paperback $9.95
LET'S US GO DOWN TO THE RIVER 'N...
by Various Authors ....paperback $9.95
MISSISSIPPI RIVER PO' FOLK
by Pat Wallace ....paperback $9.95
GHOSTS OF THE MISSISSIPPI RIVER
(from Keokuk to St. Louis)
by Bruce Carlson ....paperback $9.95
GHOSTS OF THE MISSISSIPPI RIVER
(from Dubuque to Keokuk)
by Bruce Carlson ....paperback $9.95
MAKIN' DO IN ILLINOIS
by Various Authors ....paperback $9.95
MY VERY FIRST
by Various Authors ....paperback $9.95
VACANT LOT, SCHOOL YARD & BACK ALLEY GAMES
by Various Authors ....paperback $9.95
HOW TO TALK MIDWESTERN
by Robert Thomas ....paperback $7.95

INDIANA BOOKS

HOW TO TALK HOOSIER
By Netha Bell .paperback $7.95
REVENGE OF ROADKILL
by Bruce Carlson . . . . .paperback $7.95
LET'S US GO DOWN TO THE RIVER 'N...
by Various Authors . . . . .paperback $9.95
101 WAYS TO USE A DEAD RIVER FLY
by Bruce Carlson . . . . .paperback $7.95
VACANT LOT, SCHOOL YARD & BACK ALLEY GAMES
by Various Authors . . . . .paperback $9.95
HOW TO TALK MIDWESTERN
by Robert Thomas . . . . .paperback $7.95
INDIANA PRAIRIE SKIRTS
by Bev Faaborg & Lois Brinkman . . . . .paperback $9.95
INDIANA COOKIN'
by Bruce Carlson . . . .(3x5) paperback $5.95

IOWA BOOKS

IOWA COOKIN'
by Bruce Carlson . . . .(3x5) paperback $5.95
IOWA'S ROADKILL COOKBOOK
by Bruce Carlson . . . . .paperback $7.95
REVENGE OF ROADKILL
by Bruce Carlson . . . . .paperback $7.95
GHOSTS OF THE AMANA COLONIES
by Lori Erickson . . . . .paperback $9.95
GHOSTS OF THE IOWA GREAT LAKES
by Bruce Carlson . . . . .paperback $9.95
GHOSTS OF THE MISSISSIPPI RIVER
(from Dubuque to Keokuk)
by Bruce Carlson . . . . .paperback $9.95

GHOSTS OF THE MISSISSIPPI RIVER
(from Minneapolis to Dubuque)
     by Bruce Carlson .... paperback $9.95
GHOSTS OF POLK COUNTY, IOWA
     by Tom Welch .... paperback $9.95
TALES OF HACKETT'S CREEK
     by Dan Titus .... paperback $9.95
TALL TALES OF THE MISSISSIPPI RIVER
     by Dan Titus .... paperback $9.95
101 WAYS TO USE A DEAD RIVER FLY
     by Bruce Carlson .... paperback $7.95
LET'S US GO DOWN TO THE RIVER 'N...
     by Various Authors .... paperback $9.95
TRICKS WE PLAYED IN IOWA
     by Various Authors .... paperback $9.95
IOWA, THE LAND BETWEEN THE VOWELS
(farm boy stories from the early 1900s)
     by Bruce Carlson .... paperback $9.95
LOST & BURIED TREASURE OF THE MISSISSIPPI RIVER
     by Netha Bell & Gary Scholl .... paperback $9.95
Some Pretty Tame, but Kinda Funny Stories About Early
IOWA LADIES-OF-THE-EVENING
     by Bruce Carlson .... paperback $9.95
THE VANISHING OUTHOUSE OF IOWA
     by Bruce Carlson .... paperback $9.95
IOWA'S EARLY HOME REMEDIES
     by 26 Students at Wapello Elem. School .. paperback $9.95
IOWA - A JOURNEY IN A PROMISED LAND
     by Kathy Yoder .... paperback $16.95
LOST & BURIED TREASURE OF THE MISSOURI RIVER
     by Netha Bell .... paperback $9.95
FIELD GUIDE TO IOWA'S CRITTERS
     by Bruce Carlson .... paperback $7.95
OLD IOWA HOUSES, YOUNG LOVES
     by Bruce Carlson .... paperback $9.95

SKUNK RIVER ANTHOLOGY
    by Gene Olson . . . . .paperback $9.95
VACANT LOT, SCHOOL YARD & BACK ALLEY GAMES
    by Various Authors . . . . .paperback $9.95
HOW TO TALK MIDWESTERN
    by Robert Thomas . . . . .paperback $7.95

KANSAS BOOKS

HOW TO TALK KANSAS . . . . .paperback $7.95
STOPOVER IN KANSAS
    by Jon McAlpin . . . . .paperback $9.95
LET'S US GO DOWN TO THE RIVER 'N...
    by Various Authors . . . . .paperback $9.95
LOST & BURIED TREASURE OF THE MISSOURI RIVER
    by Netha Bell .paperback $9.95
101 WAYS TO USE A DEAD RIVER FLY
    by Bruce Carlson . . . . .paperback $7.95
VACANT LOT, SCHOOL YARD & BACK ALLEY GAMES
    by Various Authors . . . . .paperback $9.95
HOW TO TALK MIDWESTERN
    by Robert Thomas . . . . .paperback $7.95

KENTUCKY BOOKS

TALES OF HACKETT'S CREEK
    by Dan Titus . . . . .paperback $9.95
LOST & BURIED TREASURE OF THE MISSISSIPPI RIVER
    by Netha Bell & Gary Scholl . . . . .paperback $9.95
LET'S US GO DOWN TO THE RIVER 'N...
    by Various Authors . . . . .paperback $9.95

101 WAYS TO USE A DEAD RIVER FLY
by Bruce Carlson . . . . .paperback $7.95
TALL TALES OF THE MISSISSIPPI RIVER
by Dan Titus . . . . .paperback $9.95
MY VERY FIRST
by Various Authors . . . . .paperback $9.95
VACANT LOT, SCHOOL YARD & BACK ALLEY GAMES
by Various Authors . . . . .paperback $9.95

MICHIGAN BOOKS

MICHIGAN COOKIN'
by Bruce Carlson . . . . .paperback $7.95
MICHIGAN'S ROADKILL COOKBOOK
by Bruce Carlson . . . . .paperback $7.95
MICHIGAN'S VANISHING OUTHOUSE
by Bruce Carlson . . . . .paperback $9.95

MINNESOTA BOOKS

MINNESOTA'S ROADKILL COOKBOOK
by Bruce Carlson . . . . .paperback $7.95
REVENGE OF ROADKILL
by Bruce Carlson . . . . .paperback $7.95
GHOSTS OF THE MISSISSIPPI RIVER
(from Minneapolis to Dubuque)
by Bruce Carlson . . . . .paperback $9.95
LAKES COUNTRY COOKBOOK
by Bruce Carlson . . . . .paperback $11.95

TALES OF HACKETT'S CREEK
        by Dan Titus . . . . .paperback $9.95
MINNESOTA'S VANISHING OUTHOUSE
        by Bruce Carlson . . . . .paperback $9.95
TALL TALES OF THE MISSISSIPPI RIVER
        by Dan Titus . . . . .paperback $9.95
Some Pretty Tame, but Kinda Funny Stories About Early
MINNESOTA LADIES-OF-THE-EVENING
        by Bruce Carlson . . . . .paperback $9.95
101 WAYS TO USE A DEAD RIVER FLY
        by Bruce Carlson . . . . .paperback $7.95
LOST & BURIED TEASURE OF THE MISSISSIPPI RIVER
        by Netha Bell & Gary Scholl . . . . .paperback $9.95
VACANT LOT, SCHOOL YARD & BACK ALLEY GAMES
        by Various Authors . . . . .paperback $9.95
HOW TO TALK MIDWESTERN
        by Robert Thomas . . . . .paperback $7.95
MINNESOTA COOKIN'
        by Bruce Carlson . . . .(3x5) paperback $5.95

MISSOURI BOOKS

MISSOURI COOKIN'
        by Bruce Carlson . . . .(3x5) paperback $5.95
MISSOURI'S ROADKILL COOKBOOK
        by Bruce Carlson . . . . .paperback $7.95
REVENGE OF THE ROADKILL
        by Bruce Carlson . . . . .paperback $7.95
LET'S US GO DOWN TO THE RIVER 'N...
        by Various Authors . . . . .paperback $9.95

LAKES COUNTRY COOKBOOK
  by Bruce Carlson ....paperback $11.95
101 WAYS TO USE A DEAD RIVER FLY
  by Bruce Carlson ....paperback $7.95
TALL TALES OF THE MISSISSIPPI RIVER
  by Dan Titus ....paperback $9.95
TALES OF HACKETT'S CREEK
  by Dan Titus ....paperback $9.95
STRANGE FOLKS ALONG THE MISSISSIPPI
  by Pat Wallace ....paperback $9.95
LOST AND BURIED TREASURE OF THE MISSOURI RIVER
  by Netha Bell ....paperback $9.95
HOW TO TALK MISSOURIAN
  by Bruce Carlson ....paperback $7.95
VACANT LOT, SCHOOL YARD & BACK ALLEY GAMES
  by Various Authors ....paperback $9.95
HOW TO TALK MIDWESTERN
  by Robert Thomas ....paperback $7.95
LOST & BURIED TREASURE OF THE MISSISSIPPI RIVER
  by Netha Bell & Gary Scholl ....paperback $9.95
MISSISSIPPI RIVER PO' FOLK
  by Pat Wallace ....paperback $9.95
Some Pretty Tame, but Kinda Funny Stories About Early
MISSOURI LADIES-OF-THE-EVENING
  by Bruce Carlson ....paperback $9.95
A FIELD GUIDE TO MISSOURI'S CRITTERS
  by Bruce Carlson ....paperback $7.95
EARLY MISSOURI HOME REMEDIES
  by Various Authors ....paperback $9.95
UNDERGROUND MISSOURI
  by Bruce Carlson ....paperpback $9.95
MISSISSIPPI RIVER COOKIN' BOOK
  by Bruce Carlson ....paperback $11.95

NEBRASKA BOOKS

LOST & BURIED TREASURE OF THE MISSOURI RIVER
by Netha Bell . . . . .paperback $9.95
101 WAYS TO USE A DEAD RIVER FLY
by Bruce Carlson . . . . .paperback $7.95
LET'S US GO DOWN TO THE RIVER 'N...
by Various Authors . . . . .paperback $9.95
HOW TO TALK MIDWESTERN
by Robert Thomas . . . . .paperback $7.95
VACANT LOT, SCHOOL YARD & BACK ALLEY GAMES
by Various Authors . . . . .paperback $9.95

TENNESSEE BOOKS

TALES OF HACKETT'S CREEK
by Dan Titus . . . . .paperback $9.95
TALL TALES OF THE MISSISSIPPI RIVER
by Dan Titus . . . . .paperback $9.95
UNSOLVED MYSTERIES OF THE MISSISSIPPI
by Netha Bell . . . . .paperback $9.95
LOST & BURIED TREASURE OF THE MISSISSIPPI RIVER
by Netha Bell & Gary Scholl . . . . .paperback $9.95
LET'S US GO DOWN TO THE RIVER 'N...
by Various Authors . . . . .paperback $9.95
101 WAYS TO USE A DEAD RIVER FLY
by Bruce Carlson . . . . .paperback $7.95
VACANT LOT, SCHOOL YARD & BACK ALLEY GAMES
by Various Authors . . . . .paperback $9.95

WISCONSIN

HOW TO TALK WISCONSIN . . . . .paperback $7.95
WISCONSIN COOKIN'
     by Bruce Carlson . . . .(3x5) paperback $5.95
WISCONSIN'S ROADKILL COOKBOOK
     by Bruce Carlson . . . . .paperback $7.95
REVENGE OF ROADKILL
     by Bruce Carlson . . . . .paperback $7.95
TALL TALES OF THE MISSISSIPPI RIVER
     by Dan Titus .paperback $9.95
LAKES COUNTRY COOKBOOK
     by Bruce Carlson . . . . .paperback $11.95
TALES OF HACKETT'S CREEK
     by Dan Titus .paperback $9.95
LET'S US GO DOWN TO THE RIVER 'N...
     by Various Authors . . . . .paperback $9.95
101 WAYS TO USE A DEAD RIVER FLY
     by Bruce Carlson . . . . .paperback $7.95
LOST & BURIED TREASURE OF THE MISSISSIPPI RIVER
     by Netha Bell & Gary Scholl . . . . .paperback $9.95
HOW TO TALK MIDWESTERN
     by Robert Thomas . . . . .paperback $7.95
VACANT LOT, SCHOOL YARD & BACK ALLEY GAMES
     by Various Authors . . . . .paperback $9.95
MY VERY FIRST
     by Various Authors . . . . .paperback $9.95
EARLY WISCONSIN HOME REMEDIES
     by Various Authors . . . . .paperback $9.95
THE VANISHING OUTHOUSE OF WISCONSIN
     by Bruce Carlson . . . . .paperback $9.95
GHOSTS OF DOOR COUNTY, WISCONSIN
     by Geri Rider .paperback $9.95

RIVER BOOKS

ON THE SHOULDERS OF A GIANT
by M. Cody and D. Walker . . . . .paperback $9.95
SKUNK RIVER ANTHOLOGY
by Gene "Will" Olson . . . . .paperback $9.95
JACK KING vs DETECTIVE MACKENZIE
by Netha Bell .paperback $9.95
LOST & BURIED TREASURE OF THE MISSISSIPPI RIVER
by Netha Bell & Gary Scholl . . . . .paperback $9.95
MISSISSIPPI RIVER PO' FOLK
by Pat Wallace . . . . .paperback $9.95
STRANGE FOLKS ALONG THE MISSISSIPPI
by Pat Wallace . . . . .paperback $9.95
TALES OF HACKETT'S CREEK
(1940s Mississippi River kids)
by Dan Titus . . . . .paperback $9.95
101 WAYS TO USE A DEAD RIVER FLY
by Bruce Carlson . . . . .paperback $7.95
LET'S US GO DOWN TO THE RIVER 'N...
by Various Authors . . . . .paperback $9.95
LOST & BURIED TREASURE OF THE MISSOURI
by Netha Bell .paperback $9.95
LIL' RED BOOK OF FISHING TIPS
by Tom Hollatz . . . . .paperback $7.95

COOKBOOKS

THE BACK-TO-THE SUPPER TABLE COOKBOOK
by Susie Babbington . . . . .paperback $11.95
THE COVERED BRIDGES COOKBOOK
by Bruce Carlson . . . . .paperback $11.95
COUNTRY COOKING-RECIPES OF MY AMISH HERITAGE
by Kathy Yoder . . . . .paperback $9.95
CIVIL WAR COOKIN', STORIES, 'N SUCH
by Darlene Funkhouser . . . . .paperback $9.95

SOUTHERN HOMEMADE
by Lorraine Lott . . . . .paperback $11.95
THE ORCHARD, BERRY PATCHES, AND GARDEN CKBK
by Bruce Carlson . . . . .paperback $11.95
THE BODY SHOP COOKBOOK
by Sherrill Wolff . . . . .paperback $14.95
CAMP COOKING COOKBOOK
by Mary Ann Kerl . . . . .paperback $9.95
FARMERS' MARKET COOKBOOK
by Bruce Carlson . . . . .paperback $9.95
HERBAL COOKERY
by Dixie Stephen . . . . .paperback $9.95
MAD ABOUT GARLIC
by Pat Reppert . . . . .paperback $9.95
BREADS! BREADS! BREADS!
by Mary Ann Kerl . . . . .paperback $9.95
PUMPKIN PATCHES, PROVERBS & PIES
by Cherie Reilly . . . . .paperback $9.95
ARIZONA COOKING
by Barbara Soden . . . . .paperback $5.95
SOUTHWEST COOKING
by Barbara Soden . . . . .paperback $5.95
EATIN' OHIO
by Rus Pishnery . . . . .paperback $9.95
EATIN' ILLINOIS
by Rus Pishnery . . . . .paperback $9.95
KENTUCKY COOKIN'
by Marilyn Tucker Carlson . . . . .paperback $5.95
INDIANA COOKIN'
by Bruce Carlson . . . . .paperback $5.95
KANSAS COOKIN'
by Bruce Carlson . . . . .paperback $5.95

NEW JERSEY COOKING
by Bruce Carlson ....paperback $5.95
NEW MEXICO COOKING
by Barbara Soden ....paperback $5.95
NEW YORK COOKIN'
by Bruce Carlson ....paperback $5.95
OHIO COOKIN'
by Bruce Carlson ....paperback $5.95
PENNSYLVANIA COOKING
by Bruce Carlson ....paperback $5.95
AMISH-MENNONITE STRAWBERRY COOKBOOK
by Alta Kauffman ....paperback $5.95
APPLES! APPLES! APPLES!
by Melissa Mosley ....paperback $5.95
APPLES GALORE!!!
by Bruce Carlson ....paperback $5.95
BERRIES! BERRIES! BERRIES!
by Melissa Mosley ....paperback $5.95
BERRIES GALORE!!!
by Bruce Carlson ....paperback $5.95
CHERRIES! CHERRIES! CHERRIES!
by Marilyn Carlson ....paperback $5.95
CITRUS! CITRUS! CITRUS!
by Lisa Nafziger ....paperback $5.95
COOKING WITH CIDER
by Bruce Carlson ....paperback $5.95
COOKING WITH THINGS THAT GO BAA
by Bruce Carlson ....paperback $5.95
COOKING WITH THINGS THAT GO CLUCK
by Bruce Carlson ....paperback $5.95
COOKING WITH THINGS THAT GO MOO
by Bruce Carlson ....paperback $5.95
COOKING WITH THINGS THAT GO OINK
by Bruce Carlson ....paperback $5.95

GARLIC! GARLIC! GARLIC!
      by Bruce Carlson ....paperback $5.95
KID COOKIN'
      by Bev Faaborg ....paperback $5.95
THE KID'S GARDEN FUN BOOK
      by Theresa McKeown ....paperback $5.95
KID'S PUMPKIN FUN BOOK
      by J. Ballhagen ....paperback $5.95
NUTS! NUTS! NUTS!
      by Melissa Mosley ....paperback $5.95
PEACHES! PEACHES! PEACHES!
      by Melissa Mosley ....paperback $5.95
PUMPKINS! PUMPKINS! PUMPKINS!
      by Melissa Mosley ....paperback $5.95
VEGGIE-FRUIT-NUT MUFFIN RECIPES
      by Darlene Funkhouser ....paperback $5.95
WORKING GIRL COOKING
      by Bruce Carlson ....paperback $5.95
SOME LIKE IT HOT!!!
      by Barbara Soden ....paperback $5.95
HOW TO COOK SALSA
      by Barbara Soden ....paperback $5.95
COOKING WITH FRESH HERBS
      by Eleanor Wagner ....paperback $5.95
BUFFALO COOKING
      by Momfeather ....paperback $5.95
NO STOVE-NO SHARP KNIFE KIDS NO-COOK COOKBOOK
      by Timmy Denning ....paperback $9.95

MISCELLANEOUS

HALLOWEEN
     by Bruce Carlson ....paperback $9.95
VEGGIE TALK
     by Glynn Singleton ....paperback $6.95
WASHASHORE
     by Margaret Potter ....paperback $9.95
PRINCES AND TOADS
     by Dr. Sharon Tobler ....paperback $12.95
HOW SOON CAN YOU GET HERE, DOC?
     by David Wynia, DVM ....paperback $9.95
MY PAW WAS A GREAT DANE
     by R. E. Rasmussen, DVM ....paperback $14.95

To order any of these books
from Quixote Press
call
1-800-571-2665